FREEDOM AND CULTURE

JOHN DEWEY

GREAT BOOKS IN PHILOSOPHY

PROMETHEUS BOOKS
Buffalo, New York

Additional Titles on Social and Political Philosophy in Prometheus's Great Books in Philosophy Series

Aristotle
The Politics

Francis Bacon
Essays

Mikhail Bakunin
*The Basic Bakunin:
Writings, 1869–1871*

Edmund Burke
*Reflections on the Revolution
in France*

G. W. F. Hegel
The Philosophy of History

Thomas Hobbes
The Leviathan

Sidney Hook
Paradoxes of Freedom

Sidney Hook
*Reason, Social Myths,
and Democracy*

John Locke
Second Treatise on Civil Government

Niccolo Machiavelli
The Prince

Karl Marx and Frederick Engels
*The Economic and Philosophical
Manuscripts of 1844* and
The Communist Manifesto

John Stuart Mill
*Considerations on
Representative Government*

John Stuart Mill
On Liberty

John Stuart Mill
On Socialism

John Stuart Mill
The Subjection of Women

Friedrich Nietzsche
Thus Spake Zarathustra

Thomas Paine
Common Sense

Thomas Paine
Rights of Man

Plato
Lysis, Phaedrus, and *Symposium*

Plato
The Republic

Jean-Jacques Rousseau
The Social Contract

Mary Wollstonecraft
A Vindication of the Rights of Women

See the back of this volume for a complete list of titles in Prometheus's Great Books in Philosophy and Great Minds series.

Published 1989 by Prometheus Books

59 John Glenn Drive, Amherst, New York 14228–2197,
716–691–0133. FAX: 716–691–0137.

Library of Congress Catalog Number: 89–62323
ISBN 0–87975–560–1

Printed in the United States of America on acid-free paper.

Written in 1939

JOHN DEWEY was born near Burlington, Vermont, on October 20, 1859. Twenty years later, he graduated from the University of Vermont, after which he taught public school in Pennsylvania and Vermont. Having become interested in philosophical questions while still an undergraduate, Dewey continued his philosophical training at Johns Hopkins University. In 1884 he was awarded a doctorate in philosophy from that institution and soon thereafter he accepted a position in philosophy at the University of Michigan. Except for a one-year appointment as professor of philosophy at the University of Minnesota, Dewey remained at Michigan—serving a five-year term as chairman—until 1894 when he moved with his wife, Alice Chipman, to the University of Chicago and began his tenure as chairman of the philosophy department. It was at Chicago that Dewey received national recognition for his pioneering work in the field of education with the development of his laboratory school in which experimental approaches to teaching were explored. After a falling out with the University of Chicago over the administration of the school, Dewey left in 1904 and accepted a professorship in philosophy at Columbia University.

For the next twenty-six years, Dewey's academic position at Columbia served as a springboard for his many and varied interests—e.g., social questions, politics, education, and public affairs—his national and international reputation found him working with such groups as the American Philosophical Association, the American Association of University Professors (founder and first president), the Teacher's Union, and the American Civil Liberties Union, among others.

Unlike those who consider retirement a time to relax and enjoy the restful pleasures of later life, John Dewey dedicated his remaining years to sorting out the tough social questions facing America and the world. He joined organizations whose goal was to increase public education in the areas of domestic and international politics. One of Dewey's most famous public forums was his participation in the commission that met in Mexico City to inquire into the charges leveled against Leon Trotsky at his Moscow trial. The commission subsequently found Trotsky innocent of the charges. He was also one of several colleagues who publicly defended fellow philosopher

Bertrand Russell when Russell was denied a teaching position at the City College of New York because of public criticism of his views on marriage and religion.

In developing his own unique philosophical stance, John Dewey overcame Hegelian idealism to embrace the pragmatic views of William James. Dewey's devotion to free inquiry and the scientific method found him spearheading the intellectual opposition against the belief that absolute knowledge can be attained in a world of variegated circumstances, discoveries, trailblazing research, and advances of all kinds. For Dewey, knowledge is not absolute, immutable, and eternal, but rather relative to the developmental interaction of man with his world as problems arise to present themselves for solution. This scientific approach, which allows one to declare the truth of a claim until—and only until—there is negative evidence sufficient to disconfirm the hypothesis, opens the mind to the need for a democratic approach to problem solving. Without cooperation and a rational tolerance for diverse points of view within a pluralistic community, society has no hope of mature development.

During his ninety-three years, John Dewey authored more than two dozen books and scores of articles in both scholarly and popular publications. He is truly America's foremost philosopher, whose work will influence intellectuals throughout the world for many years to come.

John Dewey died in New York City on June 1, 1952.

Contents

Contents

1. The Problem of Freedom

What is freedom and why is it prized? Is desire for freedom inherent in human nature or is it a product of special circumstances? Is it wanted as an end or as a means of getting other things? Does its possession entail responsibilities, and are these responsibilities so onerous that the mass of men will readily surrender liberty for the sake of greater ease? Is the struggle for liberty so arduous that most men are easily distracted from the endeavor to achieve and maintain it? Does freedom in itself and in the things it brings with it seem as important as security of livelihood; as food, shelter, clothing, or even as having a good time? Did man ever care as much for it as we in this country have been taught to believe? Is there any truth in the old notion that the driving force in political history has been the effort of the common man to achieve freedom? Was our own struggle for political independence in any genuine sense animated by desire for freedom, or were there a number of discomforts that our ancestors wanted to get rid of, things having nothing in common save that they were felt to be troublesome?

Is love of liberty ever anything more than a desire to be liberated from some special restriction? And when it is got rid of does the desire for liberty die down until something else feels intolerable? Again, how does the desire for freedom compare in intensity with the desire to feel equal with others, especially with those who have previously been called superiors? How do the fruits of liberty compare with the enjoyments that spring from a feeling of union, of solidarity, with others? Will men surrender their liberties if they believe that by so doing they will obtain the satisfaction that comes from a sense of fusion with others and that respect by others which is the product of the strength furnished by solidarity?

The present state of the world is putting questions like these to citizens of all democratic countries. It is putting them with special force to us in a country where democratic institutions have been bound up with a certain tradition, the "ideology" of which the Declaration of Independence is the classic expression. This tradition has taught us that attainment of freedom is the goal of political history; that self-government is the inherent right of free men and is that which, when it is achieved, men prize above all else. Yet as we look at the world we see supposedly free institutions in many countries not so much overthrown as abandoned willingly, apparently with enthusiasm. We may infer that what has happened is proof they never existed in reality but only in name. Or we may console ourselves with a belief that unusual conditions, such as national frustration and humiliation, have led men to welcome any kind of government that promised to restore national self-respect. But conditions in our country as well as the eclipse of democracy in other countries compel us to ask questions about the career and fate of free societies, even our own.

There perhaps was a time when the questions asked would have seemed to be mainly or exclusively political. Now we know better. For we know that a large part of the causes which have produced the conditions that are expressed in the questions is the dependence of politics upon other forces, notably the economic. The problem of the constitution of human nature is involved, since it is part of our tradition that love of freedom is inherent in its make-up. Is the popular psychology of democracy a myth? The old doctrine about human nature was also tied up with the ethical belief that political democracy is a moral right and that the laws upon which it is based are fundamental moral laws which every form of social organization should obey. If belief in natural rights and natural laws as the foundation of free government is surrendered, does the latter have any other moral basis? For while it would be foolish to believe that the American colonies fought the battles that secured their independence and that they built their government consciously and deliberately upon a foundation of psychological and moral theories, yet the democratic tradition, call it dream or call it penetrating vision, was so closely allied with beliefs about human nature and about the moral ends which political institutions should serve, that a rude shock occurs when these affiliations break down. Is there anything to take their place, anything that will give the kind of support they once gave?

The problems behind the questions asked, the forces which give the questions their urgency, go beyond the particular beliefs which formed the early psychological and moral foundation of democracy. After retiring from public office, Thomas Jefferson in his old age carried on a friendly philosophical correspondence with John Adams. In one of his letters he made a statement about existing American conditions and expressed a hope about their future estate: "The advance of liberalism encourages a hope that the human mind will some day get back to the freedom it enjoyed two thousand years ago. This country, which has given to the world the example of physical liberty, owes to it that of moral emancipation also, for as yet it is but nominal with us. The inquisition of public opinion overwhelms in practice the freedom asserted by the laws in theory." The situation that has developed since his time may well lead us to reverse the ideas he expressed, and inquire whether political freedom can be maintained without that freedom of culture which he expected to be the final result of political freedom. It is no longer easy to entertain the hope that given political freedom as the one thing necessary all other things will in time be added to it—and so to us. For we now know that the relations which exist between persons, outside of political institutions, relations of industry, of communication, of science, art and religion, affect daily associations, and thereby deeply affect the attitudes and habits expressed in government and rules of law. If it is true that the political and legal react to shape the other things, it is even more true that political institutions are an effect, not a cause.

It is this knowledge that sets the theme to be discussed. For this complex of conditions which taxes the terms upon which human beings associate and live together is summed up in the word *Culture*. The problem is to know what kind of culture is so free in itself that it conceives and begets political freedom as its accompaniment and consequence. What about the state of science and knowledge; of the arts, fine and technological; of friendships and family life; of business and finance; of the attitudes and dispositions created in the give and take of ordinary day by day associations? No matter what is the native make-up of human nature, its working activities, those which respond to institutions and rules and which finally shape the pattern of the latter, are created by the whole body of occupations, interests, skills, beliefs that constitute a given culture. As the latter changes, especially as it grows complex and intricate in the way in which American life has changed since our political organization took shape, new problems take the place of those governing the earlier formation and distribution of political powers. The view that love of freedom is so inherent in man that, if it only has a chance given it by abolition of oppressions exercised by church and state, it will produce and maintain free institutions is no longer adequate. The idea naturally arose when settlers in a new country felt that the distance they had put between themselves and the forces that oppressed them effectively symbolized everything that stood between them and permanent achievement of freedom. We are now forced to see that positive conditions, forming the prevailing state of culture, are required. Release from oppressions and repressions which previously existed marked a necessary transition, but transitions are but bridges to something different.

Early republicans were obliged even in their own time to note that general conditions, such as are summed up under the name of culture, had a good deal to do with political institutions. For they held that oppressions of state and church had exercised a corrupting influence upon human nature, so that the original impulse to liberty had either been lost or warped out of shape. This was a virtual admission that surrounding conditions may be stronger than native tendencies. It proved a degree of plasticity in human nature that required exercise of continual solicitude—expressed in the saying that eternal vigilance is the price of liberty. The Founding Fathers were aware that love of power is a trait of human nature, so strong a one that definite barriers had to be erected to keep persons who get into positions of official authority from encroachments that undermine free institutions. Admission that men may be brought by long habit to hug their chains implies a belief that second or acquired nature is stronger than original nature.

Jefferson at least went further than this. For his fear of the growth of manufacturing and trade and his preference for agrarian pursuits amounted to acceptance of the idea that interests bred by certain pursuits may fundamentally alter original human nature and the institutions that are congenial to it. That the development Jefferson dreaded has come about and to a much greater degree than he could have anticipated is an obvious fact. We face today the consequences of the fact that an agricultural and rural people has become an urban industrial population.

Proof is decisive that economic factors are an intrinsic part of the culture that determines the actual turn taken by political measures and rules, no matter what verbal beliefs are held. Although it later became the fashion to blur the connection which exists between economics and politics, and even to reprove those who called attention to it, Madison as well as Jefferson was quite aware of the connection and of its bearing upon democracy. Knowledge that the connection demanded a general distribution of property and the prevention of rise of the extremely poor and the extremely rich, was however different from explicit recognition of a relation between culture and nature so intimate that the former may shape the patterns of thought and action.

Economic relations and habits cannot be set apart in isolation any more than political institutions can be. The state of knowledge of nature, that is, of physical science, is a phase of culture upon which industry and commerce, the production and distribution of goods and the regulation of services directly depend. Unless we take into account the rise of the new science of nature in the seventeenth century and its growth to its present state, our economic agencies of production and distribution and ultimately of consumption cannot be understood. The connection of the events of the industrial revolution with those of the advancing scientific revolution is an incontrovertible witness.

It has not been customary to include the arts, the fine arts, as an important part of the social conditions that bear upon democratic institutions and personal freedom. Even after the influence of the state of industry and of natural science has been admitted, we still tend to draw the line at the idea that literature, music, painting, the drama, architecture, have any intimate connection with the cultural bases of democracy. Even those who call themselves good democrats are often content to look upon the fruits of these arts as adornments of culture rather than as things in whose enjoyment all should partake, if democracy is to be a reality. The state of things in totalitarian countries may induce us to revise this opinion. For it proves that no matter what may be the case with the impulses and powers that lead the creative artist to do his work, works of art once brought into existence are the most compelling of the means of communication by which emotions are stirred and opinions formed. The theater, the movie and music hall, even the picture gallery, eloquence, popular parades, common sports and recreative agencies, have all been brought under regulation as part of the propaganda agencies by which dictatorship is kept in power without being regarded by the masses as oppressive. We are beginning to realize that emotions and imagination are more potent in shaping public sentiment and opinion than information and reason.

Indeed, long before the present crisis came into being there was a saying that if one could control the songs of a nation, one need not care who made its laws. And historical study shows that primitive religions owe their power in determining belief and action to their ability to reach emotions and imagination by rites and ceremonies, by legend and folklore, all clothed with the traits that mark works of art. The Church that has had by far the greatest influence in the modern world took over their agencies of esthetic appeal and incorporated them into its own structure, after adapting them to its own purpose, in winning and holding the allegiance of the masses.

A totalitarian regime is committed to control of the whole life of all its subjects by its hold over feelings, desires, emotions, as well as opinions. This indeed is a mere truism, since a totalitarian state has to be total. But save as we take it into account we shall not appreciate the intensity of the revival of the warfare between state and church that exists in Germany and Russia. The conflict is not the expression of the whim of a leader. It is inherent in any regime that demands the *total* allegiance of all its subjects. It must first of all, and most enduringly of all, if it is to be permanent, command the imagination, with all the impulses and motives we have been accustomed to call *inner*. Religious organizations are those which rule by use of these means, and for that reason are an inherent competitor with any political state that sets out on the totalitarian road. Thus it is that the very things that seem to us in democratic countries the most obnoxious features of the totalitarian state are the very things for which its advocates recommend it. They are the things for whose absence they denounce democratic countries. For they say that failure to

enlist the whole make-up of citizens, emotional as well as ideological, condemns democratic states to employ merely external
and mechanical devices to hold the loyal support of its citizens.
We may regard all this as a symptom of a collective hallucination,
such as at times seems to have captured whole populations. But
even so, we must recognize the influence of this factor if we are
ourselves to escape collective delusion—that totalitarianism
rests upon external coercion alone.

Finally, the moral factor is an intrinsic part of the complex of
social forces called culture. For no matter whether or not one
shares the view, now held on different grounds by different
groups, that there is no scientific ground or warrant for moral
conviction and judgments—it is certain that human beings hold
some things dearer than they do others, and that they struggle
for the things they prize, spending time and energy in their behalf: doing so indeed to such an extent that the best measure we
have of what is valued is the effort spent in its behalf. Not only
so, but for a number of persons to form anything that can be
called a community in its pregnant sense there must be values
prized in common. Without them, any so-called social group,
class, people, nation, tends to fall apart into molecules having
but mechanically enforced connections with one another. For the
present at least we do not have to ask whether values are moral,
having a kind of life and potency of their own, or are but by-
products of the working of other conditions, biological, economic or whatever.

The qualification will indeed seem quite superfluous to most,
so habituated have most persons become to believing, at least
nominally, that moral forces are the ultimate determinants of the
rise and fall of all human societies—while religion has taught
many to believe that cosmic as well as social forces are regulated
in behalf of moral ends. The qualification is introduced, nevertheless, because of the existence of a school of philosophy holding that opinions about the values which move conduct are lacking in any scientific standing, since (according to them) the only
things that can be *known* are physical events. The denial that
values have any influence in the long run course of events is also
characteristic of the Marxist belief that forces of production ultimately control every human relationship. The idea of the impossibility of intellectual regulation of ideas and judgments about

values is shared by a number of intellectuals who have been dazzled by the success of mathematical and physical science. These last remarks suggest that there is at least one other factor in culture which needs some attention:—namely, the existence of schools of social philosophy, of competing ideologies.

The intent of the previous discussion should be obvious. The problem of freedom and of democratic institutions is tied up with the question of what kind of culture exists; with the necessity of free culture for free political institutions. The import of this conclusion extends far beyond its contrast with the simpler faith of those who formulated the democratic tradition. The question of human psychology, of the make-up of human nature in its original state, is involved. It is involved not just in a general way but with respect to its special constituents and their significance in their relations to one another. For every social and political philosophy currently professed will be found upon examination to involve a certain view about the constitution of human nature: in itself and in its relation to physical nature. What is true of this factor is true of every factor in culture, so that they need not here be listed again, although it is necessary to bear them all in mind if we are to appreciate the variety of factors involved in the problem of human freedom.

Running through the problem of the relation of this and that constituent of culture to social institutions in general and political democracy in particular is a question rarely asked. Yet it so underlies any critical consideration of the principles of each of them that some conclusion on the matter ultimately decides the position taken on each special issue. The question is whether any one of the factors is so predominant that it is *the* causal force, so that other factors are secondary and derived effects. Some kind of answer in what philosophers call a *monistic* direction has been usually given. The most obvious present example is the belief that economic conditions are ultimately the controlling forces in human relationships. It is perhaps significant that this view is comparatively recent. At the height of the eighteenth century, Enlightenment, the prevailing view, gave final supremacy to reason, to the advance of science and to education. Even during the last century, a view was held which is expressed in the motto of a certain school of historians: "History is past politics and politics is present history."

Because of the present fashion of economic explanation, this political view may now seem to have been the crotchet of a particular set of historical scholars. But, after all, it only formulated an idea consistently acted upon during the period of the formation of national states. It is possible to regard the present emphasis upon economic factors as a sort of intellectual revenge taken upon its earlier all but total neglect. The very word "political economy" suggests how completely economic considerations were once subordinated to political. The book that was influential in putting an end to this subjection, Adam Smith's *Wealth of Nations,* continued in its title, though not its contents, the older tradition. In the Greek period, we find that Aristotle makes the political factor so controlling that all normal economic activities are relegated to the household, so that all morally justifiable economic practice is literally domestic economy. And in spite of the recent vogue of the Marxist theory, Oppenheimer has produced a considerable body of evidence in support of the thesis that political states are the result of military conquests in which defeated people have become subjects of their conquerors, who, by assuming rule over the conquered, begot the first political states.

The rise of totalitarian states cannot, because of the bare fact of their totalitarianism, be regarded as mere reversions to the earlier theory of supremacy of the political institutional factor. Yet as compared with theories that had subordinated the political to the economic, whether in the Marxist form or in that of the British classical school, it marks reversion to ideas and still more to practices which it was supposed had disappeared forever from the conduct of any modern state. And the practices have been revived and extended with the benefit of scientific technique of control of industry, finance and commerce in ways which show the earlier governmental officials who adopted "mercantile" economics in the interest of government were the veriest bunglers at their professed job.

The idea that morals ought to be, even if it is not, the supreme regulator of social affairs is not so widely entertained as it once was, and there are circumstances which support the conclusion that when moral forces were as influential as they were supposed to be it was because morals were identical with customs which happened in fact to regulate the relations of human beings with one another. However, the idea is still advanced by sermons from the pulpit and editorials from the press that adoption of say the

Golden Rule would speedily do away with all social discord and trouble; and as I write the newspapers report the progress of a campaign for something called "moral re-armament." Upon a deeper level, the point made about the alleged identity of ethics with established customs raises the question whether the effect of the disintegration of customs that for a long time held men together in social groups can be overcome save by development of new generally accepted traditions and customs. This development, upon this view, would be equivalent to the creation of a new ethics.

However, such questions are here brought up for the sake of the emphasis they place upon the question already raised: Is there any one factor or phase of culture which is dominant, or which tends to produce and regulate others, or are economics, morals, art, science, and so on only so many aspects of the interaction of a number of factors, each of which acts upon and is acted upon by the others? In the professional language of philosophy: shall our point of view be monistic or pluralistic? The same question recurs moreover about each one of the factors listed:—about economics, about politics, about science, about art. I shall here illustrate the point by reference not to any of these things but to theories that have at various times been influential about the make-up of human nature. For these psychological theories have been marked by serious attempts to make some one constituent of human nature *the* source of motivation of action; or at least to reduce all conduct to the action of a small number of alleged native "forces." A comparatively recent example was the adoption by the classic school of economic theory of self-interest as the main motivating force of human behavior; an idea linked up on its technical side with the notion that pleasure and pain are the causes and the ends-in-view of all conscious human conduct, in desire to obtain one and avoid the other. Then there was a view that self-interest and sympathy are the two components of human nature, as opposed and balanced centrifugal and centripetal tendencies are the moving forces of celestial nature.

Just now the favorite ideological psychological candidate for control of human activity is love of power. Reasons for its selection are not far to seek. Success of search for economic profit turned out to be largely conditioned in fact upon possession of superior power while success reacted to increase power. Then the rise of national states has been attended by such vast and flagrant organization of military and naval force that politics have become more and more markedly power-politics, leading to the conclusion that there is not any other kind, although in the past the power-element has been more decently and decorously covered up. One interpretation of the Darwinian struggle for existence and survival of the fittest was used as ideological support; and some writers, notably Nietzsche (though not in the crude form often alleged), proposed an ethics of power in opposition to the supposed Christian ethics of sacrifice.

Because human nature is the factor which in one way or another is always interacting with environing conditions in production of culture, the theme receives special attention later. But the shift that has occurred from time to time in theories that have gained currency about the "ruling motive" in human nature suggests a question which is seldom asked. It is the question whether these psychologies have not in fact taken the cart to be the horse. Have they not gathered their notion as to the ruling element in human nature from observation of tendencies that are marked in contemporary collective life, and then bunched these tendencies together in some alleged psychological "force" as their cause? It is significant that human nature was taken to be strongly moved by an inherent love of freedom at the time when there was a struggle for representative government; that the motive of self-interest appeared when conditions in England enlarged the role of money, because of new methods of industrial production; that the growth of organized philanthropic activities brought sympathy into the psychological picture, and that events today are readily converted into love of power as the mainspring of human action.

In any case, the idea of culture that has been made familiar by the work of anthropological students points to the conclusion that whatever are the native constituents of human nature, the culture of a period and group is the determining influence in their arrangement; it is that which determines the patterns of behavior that mark out the activities of any group, family, clan, people, sect, faction, class. It is at least as true that the state of culture determines the order and arrangement of native tendencies as that human nature produces any particular set or system of social phenomena so as to obtain satisfaction for itself. The problem is to find out the way in which the elements of a culture interact with each other and the way in which the elements of human nature are caused to interact with one another under conditions set by their interaction with the existing environment. For example, if our American culture is largely a pecuniary culture, it is not because the original or innate structure of human nature tends of itself to obtaining pecuniary profit. It is rather that a certain complex culture stimulates, promotes and consolidates native tendencies so as to produce a certain pattern of desires and purposes. If we take all the communities, peoples, classes, tribes and nations that ever existed, we may be sure that since human nature in its native constitution is the relative constant, it cannot be appealed to, in isolation, to account for the multitude of diversities presented by different forms of association.

Primitive peoples for reasons that are now pretty evident attribute magical qualities to blood. Popular beliefs about race and inherent race differences have virtually perpetuated the older superstitions. Anthropologists are practically all agreed that the differences we find in different "races" are not due to anything in inherent physiological structure but to the effects exercised upon members of various groups by the cultural conditions under which they are reared; conditions that act upon raw or original human nature unremittingly from the very moment of birth. It has always been known that infants, born without ability in any language, come to speak the language, whatever it may be, of the community in which they were born. Like most uniform phenomena the fact aroused no curiosity and led to no generalization about the influence of cultural conditions. It was taken for granted; as a matter of course it was so "natural" as to appear inevitable. Only since the rise of systematic inquiries carried on by anthropological students has it been noted that the conditions of culture which bring about the common language of a given group produce other traits they have in common;—traits which like the mother tongue differentiate one group or society from others.

Culture as a complex body of customs tends to maintain itself. It can reproduce itself only through effecting certain differential changes in the original or native constitutions of its members.

Each culture has its own pattern, its own characteristic arrangement of its constituent energies. By the mere force of its existence as well as by deliberately adopted methods systematically pursued, it perpetuates itself through transformation of the raw or original human nature of those born immature.

These statements do not signify that biological heredity and native individual differences are of no importance. They signify that as they operate within a given social form, they are shaped and take effect *within* that particular form. They are not indigenous traits that mark off one people, one group, one class, from another, but mark differences in every group. Whatever the "white man's burden," it was not imposed by heredity.

We have traveled a seemingly long way from the questions with which we set out, so that it may appear that they had been forgotten on the journey. But the journey was undertaken for the sake of finding out something about the nature of the problem that is expressed in the questions asked. The maintenance of democratic institutions is not such a simple matter as was supposed by some of the Founding Fathers—although the wiser among them realized how immensely the new political experiment was favored by external circumstances—like the ocean that separated settlers from the governments that had an interest in using the colonists for their own purposes; the fact that feudal institutions had been left behind; that so many of the settlers had come here to escape restrictions upon religious beliefs and form of worship; and especially the existence of a vast territory with free land and immense unappropriated natural resources.

The function of culture in determining what elements of human nature are dominant and their pattern or arrangement in connection with one another goes beyond any special point to which attention is called. It affects the very idea of individuality. The idea that human nature is inherently and exclusively individual is itself a product of a cultural individualistic movement. The idea that mind and consciousness are intrinsically individual did not even occur to any one for much the greater part of human history. It would have been rejected as the inevitable source of disorder and chaos if it had occurred to anyone to suggest it:— not that their ideas of human nature on that account were any better than later ones but that they also were functions of culture. All that we can safely say is that human nature, like other forms of life, tends to differentiation, and this moves in the direction of the distinctively individual, and that it also tends toward combination, association. In the lower animals, physical-biological factors determine which tendency is dominant in a given animal or plant species and the ratio existing between the two factors—whether, for example, insects are what students call "solitary" or "social." With human beings, cultural conditions replace strictly physical ones. In the earlier periods of human history they acted almost like physiological conditions as far as deliberate intention was concerned. They were taken to be "natural" and change in them to be unnatural. At a later period the cultural conditions were seen to be subject in some degree to deliberate formation. For a time radicals then identified their policies with the belief that if only artificial social conditions could be got rid of human nature would produce almost automatically a certain kind of social arrangements, those which would give it free scope in its supposed exclusively individual character.

Tendencies toward sociality, such as sympathy, were admitted. But they were taken to be traits of an individual isolated by nature, quite as much as, say, a tendency to combine with others in order to get protection against something threatening one's own private self. Whether complete identification of human nature with individuality would be desirable or undesirable if it existed is an idle academic question. For it does not exist. Some cultural conditions develop the psychological constituents that lead toward differentiation; others stimulate those which lead in the direction of the solidarity of the beehive or anthill. The human problem is that of securing the development of each constituent so that it serves to release and mature the other. Cooperation—called fraternity in the classic French formula—is as much a part of the democratic ideal as is personal initiative. That cultural conditions were allowed to develop (markedly so in the economic phase) which subordinated cooperativeness to liberty and equality serves to explain the decline in the two latter. Indirectly, this decline is responsible for the present tendency to give a bad name to the very word *individualism* and to make *sociality* a term of moral honor beyond criticism. But that association of nullities on even the largest scale would constitute a realization of human nature is as absurd as to suppose that the latter can take place in beings whose only relations to one another are those entered into in behalf of exclusive private advantage.

The problem of freedom of cooperative individualities is then a problem to be viewed in the context of culture. The state of culture is a state of interaction of many factors, the chief of which are law and politics, industry and commerce, science and technology, the arts of expression and communication, and of morals, or the values men prize and the ways in which they evaluate them; and finally, though indirectly, the system of general ideas used by men to justify and to criticize the fundamental conditions under which they live, their social philosophy. We are concerned with the problem of freedom rather than with solutions: in the conviction that solutions are idle until the problem has been placed in the context of the elements that constitute culture as they interact with elements of native human nature. The fundamental postulate of the discussion is that isolation of any one factor, no matter how strong its workings at a given time, is fatal to understanding and to intelligent action. Isolations have abounded, both on the side of taking some one thing in human nature to be a supreme "motive" and in taking some one form of social activity to be supreme. Since the problem is here thought of as that of the ways in which a great number of factors within and without human nature interact, our next task is to ask concerning the reciprocal connections raw human nature and culture bear to one another.

2. Culture and Human Nature

In the American as in the English liberal tradition, the idea of freedom has been connected with the idea of individuality, of *the* individual. The connection has been so close and so often reiterated that it has come to seem inherent. Many persons will be surprised if they hear that freedom has ever been supposed to have another source and foundation than the very nature of individuality. Yet in the continental European tradition the affiliation of the idea of freedom is with the idea of rationality. Those are free who govern themselves by the dictates of reason; those who follow the promptings of appetite and sense are so ruled by them as to be unfree. Thus it was that Hegel at the very time he was glorifying the State wrote a philosophy of history according to which the movement of historical events was from the despotic state of the Oriental World in which only one was free to the era dawning in Germany in the Western World in which *all* are free. The same difference in contexts that give freedom its meaning is found when representatives of totalitarian Germany at the present time claim their regime is giving the subjects of their state a "higher" freedom than can be found in democratic states, individuals in the latter being unfree because their lives are chaotic and undisciplined. The aroma of the continental tradition hangs about the sayings of those who settle so many social problems to their own satisfaction by invoking a distinction between liberty and license, identifying the former with "liberty under law"—for in the classic tradition law and reason are related as child and parent. So far as the saying assigns to law an origin and authority having nothing to do with freedom, so far, that is, as it affirms the impossibility of free conditions determining their own law, it points directly, even if unintentionally, to the totalitarian state.

We do not, however, have to go as far abroad as the European continent to note that freedom has had its practical significance fixed in different ways in different cultural contexts. For in the early nineteenth century there was a great practical difference between the English and the American theories, although both associated freedom with qualities that cause human beings to be *individuals* in the distinctive sense of that word. The contrast is so flat that it would be amusing if it were not so instructive. Jefferson, who was the original and systematic promulgator of the doctrine of free, self-governing institutions, found that the properties of individuals with which these institutions were most closely associated were traits found in the farming class. In his more pessimistic moments he even went so far as to anticipate that the development of manufacturing and commerce would produce a state of affairs in which persons in this country "would eat one another" as they did in Europe. In England, on the other hand, landed proprietors were the great enemy of the new freedom, which was connected in its social and political manifestations with the activities and aims of the manufacturing class.

It is not, of course, the bare fact of contrast which is instructive but the causes for its existence. They are not far to seek. Landed proprietors formed the aristocracy in Great Britain. The hold landed interests had over law-making bodies due to feudalism was hostile to the development of manufacturing and commerce. In the United States traces of feudalism were so faint that laws against primogeniture were about all that was needed to erase them. It was easy in this country to idealize the farmers as the sturdy yeomanry who embodied all the virtues associated with the original Anglo-Saxon love of liberty, the Magna Charta, and the struggle against the despotism of the Stuarts. Farmers were the independent self-supporting class that had no favors to ask from anybody, since they were not dependent for their livelihood nor their ideas upon others, owning and managing their own farms. It is a history that again would be amusing, were it not instructive, to find that as this country changed from an agrarian one to an urban industrial one, the qualities of initiative, invention, vigor and intrinsic contribution to progress which British *laissez-faire* liberalism had associated with manufacturing pursuits were transferred by American Courts and by the politi-

cal representatives of business and finance from Jeffersonian individuals and given to the entrepreneurs who were individuals in
the British sense.

In such considerations as these—which would be reinforced
by an extensive survey of the history of the meaning given to freedom under different conditions—we have one instance and an
important one of the relation of culture to the whole problem of
freedom. The facts fall directly in line with the conclusion of the
previous chapter:—a conclusion summed up in saying that the
idea of Culture, which has become a central idea of anthropology, has such a wide sociological application that it puts a new
face upon the old, old problem of the relation of the individual
and the social. The idea of culture even outlaws the very terms in
which the problem has been conceived, independently of its
effect upon solutions proposed. For most statements of the problem have been posed as if there were some inherent difference
amounting to opposition between what is called the individual
and the social. As a consequence there was a tendency for those
who were interested in theory to line up in two parties, which at
the poles were so far apart that one denied whatever the other
asserted. One party held that social conventions, traditions, institutions, rules are maintained only by some form of coercion,
overt or covert, which encroaches upon the natural freedom of
individuals; while the other school held that individuals are such
by nature that the one standing social problem is the agencies by
which recalcitrant individuals are brought under social control
or "socialized." The term of honor of one school has been that of
reproach of the other. The two extremes serve to define the terms
in which the problem was put. Most persons occupy an intermediate and compromise position, one whose classic expression
is that the basic problem of law and politics is to find the line
which separates legitimate liberty from the proper exercise of law
and political authority, so that each can maintain its own province under its own jurisdiction; law operating only when liberty
oversteps its proper bounds, an operation supposed, during the
heights of *laissez-faire* liberalism, to be legitimate only when police action was required to keep the peace.

Few persons today hold the extreme view of Hobbes, according to which human nature is so inherently anti-social that only
experiences of the evil consequences of the war of all against all,

reigning when human nature has free play, leads men, in connection with the motive of fear, to submit to authority—human nature even then remaining so intractable that the only assurance of safety against its marauding instincts is subjection to sovereignty. But in reading books on sociology it is still not uncommon to find the basic problem stated as if it were to list and analyze agencies by which individuals are tamed or "socialized." The chief difference of these writers from Hobbes consists in the fact that much less emphasis is laid upon merely political pressure, while it is recognized that there are tendencies in original human nature which render it amenable to social rules and regulations. As a result of the successful struggle of the new industrial class in England against the restrictions which existed even after the disappearance of feudalism in its grosser obvious forms, the favorite formula weighted the scales on the side of liberty, holding that each person was free as long as his actions did not restrict the freedom of others. The latter question, moreover, was never decided by going into the concrete consequences produced by the action of one person upon other persons. It was settled by a formal legal principle such as the equal right of every sane individual of a certain age to enter into contractual relations with others—no matter whether actual conditions gave equally free scope of action on both sides or made "free" contract a jughandled affair.

However, the purpose is not to thrash over the old straw of these issues or similar issues on the moral side such as the respective parts of altruistic and egoistic tendencies in human nature. The point concerns the situation in which the problems were envisaged; the context of ideas in which as problems they were placed irrespective of the solution reached. With the intellectual resources now available, we can see that such opinions about the inherent make-up of human nature neglected the fundamental question of how its constituents are stimulated and inhibited, intensified and weakened; how their pattern is determined by interaction with cultural conditions. In consequence of this failure the views held regarding human nature were those appropriate to the purposes and policies a given group wanted to carry through. Those who wished to justify the exercise of authority over others took a pessimistic view of the constitution of human nature; those who wanted relief from something oppressive discovered

qualities of great promise in its native makeup. There is here a
field which has hardly been entered by intellectual explorers:—
the story of the way in which ideas put forth about the makeup
of human nature, ideas supposed to be the results of psychological inquiry, have been in fact only reflections of practical measures that different groups, classes, factions wished to see continued in existence or newly adopted, so that what passed as
psychology was a branch of political doctrine.

We are thus brought back to the earlier statement of principle.
The primary trouble has been that issues have been formulated as
if they were matters of the structure of human beings on one side
and of the very nature of social rules and authority on the other
side, when in reality the underlying issue is that of the relation
of the "natural" and the "cultural." Rousseau's attack upon the
arts and sciences (as well as upon existing law and government)
shocked his eighteenth century contemporaries, since the things
he claimed to be operating to corrupt human nature, by creating
inequality, were the very things they relied upon to generate un-
ending human progress. Nevertheless, he stated, in a way, the
problem of culture versus nature; putting, himself, all emphasis
upon and giving all advantage to human nature; since to him, in
spite of its raw unrefined condition, it retained its natural good-
ness as long as loss of original equality had not produced conditions that corrupted it. Kant and his German successors took up
the challenge presented in the unpopular paradoxes of Rousseau.
They tried to reverse his position; they interpreted all history as
the continuing process of culture by which the original animal
nature of man becomes refined and is transformed from the animal into the distinctively human.

But Rousseau and his opponents carried over into their discussion of the problem in its new form many of the elements derived
from the traditional way of putting it. In German philosophy, the
issue was further complicated by the rise of Nationalism which
followed the encroachments of Napoleon. Though the Germans
were defeated in war, in culture they were to be superior—an
idea that still persists in the use of *Kultur* in German nationalistic
propaganda, since superiority in culture gives the kind of rightful
authority over peoples of less culture that the human has over the
animal. The French Revolution, as well as the writings of Rousseau, had the effect, in addition, of identifying in the minds of

German thinkers the cause of culture with that of law and authority. The individual freedom, which was the "natural right" of mankind according to the philosophers of the Revolution, was to the German philosophers of the reaction but the freedom of primitive sensuous animality. A period of subjection to universal law, expressing the higher non-natural essence of humanity, was required to bring about a condition of "higher" and true freedom. Events in Germany, including the rise of totalitarianism, since the time this view was formulated, have borne the stamp of this idea. Anticipation of the existence of some ultimate and a final social state, different from original "natural" freedom and from present subordination, has played a role in all social philosophies—like the Marxist—framed under German intellectual influences. It has had the function once exercised by the idea of the Second Coming.

In no case, however, could the problem have taken its new form without the material made available by anthropological research. For what has been disclosed about the immense variety of cultures shows that the problem of the relation of individuals and their freedom to social convention, custom, tradition and rules has been stated in a wholesale form, and hence not capable of intelligent and scientific attack. Judged by the methods of the natural sciences, the procedure in the social field has been pre-scientific and anti-scientific. For science has developed by analytic observation, and by interpretations of observed facts on the basis of their relations to one another. Social theory has operated on the basis of general "forces," whether those of inherent natural "motives" or those alleged to be social.

Were it not for the inertia of habit (which applies to opinion as well as to overt acts) it would be astonishing to find today writers who are well acquainted with the procedure of physical science and yet appeal to "forces" in explanation of human and social phenomena. For in the former case, they are aware that electricity, heat, light, etc., are names for ways in which definite observable concrete phenomena behave in relation to one another, and that all description and explanation have to be made in terms of verifiable relations of observed singular events. They know that reference to electricity or heat, etc., is but a shorthand reference to relations between events which have been established by investigation of actual occurrences. But in the field of social phenomena they do not hesitate to explain concrete phenomena by reference to motives as forces (such as love of power), although these so-called forces are but reduplication, in the medium of abstract words, of the very phenomena to be explained.

Statement in terms of the relations of culture and nature to one another takes us away from vague abstractions and glittering generalities. Approach in its terms compels attention to go to the variety of cultures that exist and to the variety of constituents of human nature, including native differences between one human being and another—differences which are not just differences in quantity. The business of inquiry is with the ways in which specified constituents of human nature, native or already modified, *interact* with specified definite constituents of a given culture; conflicts and agreements between human nature on one side and social customs and rules on the other being *products* of specifiable modes of interaction. In a given community some individuals are in practical agreement with its existing institutions and others are in revolt—varying from a condition of moderate irritation and discontent to one of violent rebellion. The resulting differences when they are sufficiently marked to be labelled are the sources of the names conservative and radical, forward-looking or progressive and reactionary, etc. They cut across economic classes. For even revolutionaries have to admit that part of their problem is to create in an oppressed class consciousness of their servitude so as to arouse active protest.

This fact, so patent to even superficial observation, is sufficient disproof of the notion that the problem can be stated as one of the relation of *the* individual and *the* social, as if these names stood for any actual existences. It indicates that *ways of interaction* between human nature and cultural conditions are the first and the fundamental thing to be examined, and that the problem is to ascertain the effects of interactions between different components of different human beings and different customs, rules, traditions, institutions—the things called "social." A fallacy has controlled the traditional statement of the problem. It took results, good or bad—or both—of specific interactions as if they were original causes, on one side or the other, of what existed or else of what should exist.

It is just as certain, for example, that slaves have at times been contented with their estate of servitude as that a slave class has existed. It is certain that persons who have personally experienced no discomfort—except that commonly called moral—from existing conditions of oppression and injustice have been leaders in campaigns for equality and freedom. It is just as certain that inherent so-called social "instincts" have led men to form criminal gangs marked by certain mutual loyalties as that they have led men to cooperative activities. Now analytic observation of actual interactions to determine the elements operative on each side and their consequences is not easy in any case to execute. But recognition of its necessity is the condition of adequate judgment of actual events. Estimate of the value of any proposed policy is held back by taking the problem as if it were one of individual "forces" on one side and of social forces on the other, the nature of the forces being known in advance. We must start from another set of premises if we are to put the problem of freedom in the context where it belongs.

The questions which are asked at the beginning of the last chapter are genuine questions. But they are not questions in the abstract and cannot be discussed in a wholesale way. They are questions that demand discussion of cultural conditions, conditions of science, art, morals, religion, education and industry, so as to discover which of them in actuality promote and which retard the development of the native constituents of human nature. If we want individuals to be free we must see to it that suitable conditions exist:—a truism which at least indicates the direction in which to look and move.

It tells us among other things to get rid of the ideas that lead us to believe that democratic conditions automatically maintain themselves, or that they can be identified with fulfillment of prescriptions laid down in a constitution. Beliefs of this sort merely divert attention from what is going on, just as the patter of the prestidigitator enables him to do things that are not noticed by those whom he is engaged in fooling. For what is actually going on may be the formation of conditions that are hostile to any kind of democratic liberties. This would be too trite to repeat were it not that so many persons in the high places of business talk as if they believed or could get others to believe that the observance of formulae that have become ritualistic are effective safeguards of our democratic heritage. The same principle warns us to beware of supposing that totalitarian states are brought

about by factors so foreign to us that "It can't happen here";—
to beware especially of the belief that these states rest only upon
unmitigated coercion and intimidation. For in spite of the wide
use of purges, executions, concentration camps, deprivation of
property and of means of livelihood, no regime can endure long
in a country where a scientific spirit has once existed unless it
has the support of so-called idealistic elements in the human constitution. There is a tendency in some quarters to treat remarks
of this sort as if they were a sort of apology or justification of
dictatorships and totalitarian states. This way of reacting to an
attempt to find out what it is that commends, at least for a
time, totalitarian conditions to persons otherwise intelligent and
honorable, is dangerous. It puts hate in place of attempt at understanding; hate once aroused can be directed by skillful manipulation against other objects than those which first aroused it. It
also leads us to think that we are immune from the disease to
which others have given way so long as the evil things we see in
totalitarianism are not known to be developing among us. The
belief that only such things operate to harm democracy keeps us
from being on our guard against the causes that may be at work
undermining the values we nominally prize. It even leads us to
ignore beams in our own eyes such as our own racial prejudices.

It is extremely difficult at a distance to judge just what are the
appeals made to better elements in human nature by, say, such
policies as form the Nazi faith. We may believe that aside from
appeal to fear; from desire to escape responsibilities imposed by
free citizenship; from impulses to submission strengthened by
habits of obedience bred in the past; from desire for compensa-
tion for past humiliations, and from the action of nationalistic
sentiments growing in intensity for over a century (and not in
Germany alone), there is also love for novelty which in this particular case has taken the form of idealistic faith, among the
youth in particular, of being engaged in creating a pattern for
new institutions which the whole world will in time adopt. For
one of the elements of human nature that is often discounted in
both idea and practice is the satisfaction derived from a sense of
sharing in creative activities; the satisfaction increasing in direct
ratio to the scope of the constructive work engaged in.

Other causes may be mentioned, though with the admission
that it is quite possible in good faith to doubt or deny their

operation. There is the satisfaction that comes from a sense of union with others, a feeling capable of being intensified till it becomes a mystical sense of fusion with others and being mistaken for love on a high level of manifestation. The satisfaction obtained by the sentiment of communion with others, of the breaking down of barriers, will be intense in the degree in which it has previously been denied opportunity to manifest itself. The comparative ease with which provincial loyalties, which in Germany had been at least as intense and as influential as state-rights sentiments ever were in this country, were broken down; the similar ease, though less in degree, with which habitual religious beliefs and practices were subordinated to a feeling of racial and social union, would seem to testify that underneath there was yearning for emotional fusion. Something of this kind showed itself in most countries when they were engaged in the World War. For the time being it seemed as if barriers that separated individuals from one another had been swept away. Submission to abolition of political parties and to abolition of labor unions which had had great power, would hardly have come about so readily had there not been some kind of a void which the new regime promised to fill. Just how far the fact of uniformity is accompanied by a sense of equality in a nation where class distinctions had been rigid, one can only guess at. But there is considerable ground for believing that it has been a strong factor in reconciling "humbler" folk to enforced deprivation of material benefits, so that, at least for a time, a sense of honorable equality more than compensates for less to eat, harder and longer hours of work—since it is psychologically true that man does not live by bread alone.

It might seem as if belief in operation of "idealistic" factors was contradicted by the cruel persecutions that have taken place, things indicative of a reign of sadism rather than of desire for union with others irrespective of birth and locale. But history shows that more than once social unity has been promoted by the presence, real or alleged, of some hostile group. It has long been a part of the technique of politicians who wish to maintain themselves in power to foster the idea that the alternative is the danger of being conquered by an enemy. Nor does what has been suggested slur over in any way the effect of powerful and unremitting propaganda. For the intention has been to indicate some of the conditions whose interaction produces the social spec-

tacle. Other powerful factors in the interaction are those technologies produced by modern science which have multiplied the
means of modifying the dispositions of the mass of the population; and which, in conjunction with economic centralization,
have enabled mass opinion to become like physical goods a
matter of mass production. Here also is both a warning and a
suggestion to those concerned with cultural conditions which
will maintain democratic freedom. The warning is obvious as to
the role of propaganda, which now operates with us in channels
less direct and less official. The suggestion is that the printing
press and radio have made the problem of the intelligent and
honest use of means of communication in behalf of openly de-
clared public ends a matter of fundamental concern.

What has been said is stated by way of illustration, and it may,
if any one desires, be treated as hypothetical. For even so, the
suggestions serve to enforce the point that a social regime can
come into enduring existence only as it satisfies some elements of
human nature not previously afforded expression. On the other
hand getting relief from saturation of elements that have become
stale makes almost anything welcome if only it is different. The
general principle holds even if the elements that are provided a
new outlet are the baser things in human nature: fear, suspicion,
jealousy, inferiority complexes; factors that were excited by earlier conditions but that are now given channels of fuller expression. Common observation, especially of the young, shows that
nothing is more exasperating and more resented than stirring up
certain impulses and tendencies and then checking their manifestation. We should also note that a period of uncertainty and
insecurity, accompanied as it is by more or less unsettlement and
disturbance, creates a feeling that anything would be better than
what exists, together with desire for order and stability upon almost any terms—the latter being a reason why revolutions are
so regularly followed by reaction, and explain the fact that Lenin
expressed by saying revolutions are authoritative, though not for
the reason he gave.

Just which of these factors are involved in our own maintenance of democratic conditions or whether any of them are so
involved is, at this juncture, not so pertinent as is the principle
they illustrate. Negatively speaking, we have to get away from the
influence of belief in bald single forces, whether they are thought

of as intrinsically psychological or sociological. This includes getting away from mere hatred of abominable things, and it also means refusing to fall back on such a generalized statement as that Fascist institutions are expressions of the sort of thing to be expected in a stage of contracting capitalism, since they are a kind of final spasm of protest against approaching dissolution. We cannot reject out of hand any cause assigned; it may have some truth. But the primary need is to escape from wholesale reasons, as totalitarian as are the states ruled by dictators. We have to analyze conditions by observations, which are as discriminating as they are extensive, until we discover specific interactions that are taking place, and learn to think in terms of interactions instead of force. We are led to search even for the conditions which have given the interacting factors the power they possess.

The lesson is far from being entirely new. The founders of American political democracy were not so naively devoted to pure theory that they were unaware of the necessity of cultural conditions for the successful working of democratic forms. I could easily fill pages from Thomas Jefferson in which he insists upon the necessity of a free press, general schooling and local neighborhood groups carrying on, through intimate meetings and discussions, the management of their own affairs, if political democracy was to be made secure. These sayings could be backed up by almost equally numerous expressions of his fears for the success of republican institutions in South American countries that had thrown off the Spanish yoke.

He expressly set forth his fear that their traditions were such that domestic military despotisms would be substituted for foreign subjugations. A background of "ignorance, bigotry and superstition" was not a good omen. On one occasion he even went so far as to suggest that the best thing that could happen would be for the South American states to remain under the nominal supremacy of Spain, under the collective guarantee of France, Russia, Holland and the United States, until experience in self-government prepared them for complete independence.

The real source of the weakness that has developed later in the position of our democratic progenitors is not that they isolated the problem of freedom from the positive conditions that would nourish it, but that they did not—and in their time could not—

carry their analysis far enough. The outstanding examples of this inability are their faith in the public press and in schooling. They certainly were not wrong in emphasizing the need of a free press and of common public schools to provide conditions favorable to democracy. But to them the enemy of freedom of the press was official governmental censorship and control; they did not foresee the non-political causes that might restrict its freedom, nor the economic factors that would put a heavy premium on centralization. And they failed to see how education in literacy could become a weapon in the hands of an oppressive government, nor that the chief cause for promotion of elementary education in Europe would be increase of military power.

The inefficacy of education in general, that is, apart from constant attention to all the elements of its constitution, is illustrated in Germany itself. Its schools were so efficient that the country had the lowest rate of illiteracy in the world, the scholarship and scientific researches of its universities were known throughout the civilized globe. In fact it was not so many years ago that a distinguished American educator held them up as models to be followed in this country if the weaknesses of our higher institutions were to be remedied. Nevertheless German lower schools furnished the intellectual fodder for totalitarian propaganda, and the higher schools were the centres of reaction against the German Republic.

The illustrations are simple, and perhaps too familiar to carry much force. Nevertheless they proclaim that while free institutions over a wide territory are not possible without a mechanism, like the press, for quick and extensive communication of ideas and information, and without general literacy to take advantage of the mechanism, yet these very factors create a problem for a democracy instead of providing a final solution. Aside from the fact that the press may distract with trivialities or be an agent of a faction, or be an instrument of inculcating ideas in support of the hidden interest of a group or class (all in the name of public interest), the wide-world present scene is such that individuals are overwhelmed and emotionally confused by publicized reverberation of isolated events. And after a century of belief that the Common School system was bound by the very nature of its work to be what its earlier apostles called a "pillar of the republic," we are learning that everything about the public schools, its official agencies of control, organization and administration, the status of teachers, the subjects taught and methods of teaching them, the prevailing modes of discipline, set *problems;* and that the problems have been largely ignored as far as the relation of schools to democratic institutions is concerned. In fact the attention these things have received from various technical standpoints has been one reason why the central question has been obscured.

After many centuries of struggle and following of false gods, the natural sciences now possess methods by which particular facts and general ideas are brought into effective cooperation with one another. But with respect to means for understanding social events, we are still living in the pre-scientific epoch, although the events to be understood are the consequences of application of scientific knowledge to a degree unprecedented in history. With respect to information and understanding of social events, our state is that on one side of an immense number of undigested and unrelated facts, reported in isolation (and hence easily colored by some twist of interest) and large untested generalizations on the other side.

The generalizations are so general in the sense of remoteness from the events to which they are supposed to apply that they are matters of opinion, and frequently the rallying cries and slogans of factions and classes. They are often expressions of partisan desire clothed in the language of intellect. As matters of opinion, they are batted hither and yon in controversy and are subject to changes of popular fashion. They differ at practically every point from scientific generalizations, since the latter express the relations of facts to one another and, as they are employed to bring together more facts, are tested by the material to which they are applied.

If a glance at an editorial page of a newspaper shows what is meant by untested opinions put forth in the garb of the general principles of sound judgment, the items of the news columns illustrate what is meant by a multitude of diverse unrelated facts. The popular idea of "sensational," as it is derived from the daily press, is more instructive as to meaning of *sensations* than is the treatment accorded that subject in books on psychology. Events are sensational in the degree in which they make a strong impact in isolation from the relations to other events that give them their significance. They appeal to those who like things raw. Ordinary reports of murders, love nests, etc., are of this sort, with an artificial intensity supplied by unusual size or color of type. To say that a response is intellectual, not sensational, in the degree in which its significance is supplied by relations to other things is to state a truism. They are two sets of words used to describe the same thing.

One effect of literacy under existing conditions has been to create in a large number of persons an appetite for the momentary "thrills" caused by impacts that stimulate nerve endings but whose connections with cerebral functions are broken. Then stimulation and excitation are not so ordered that intelligence is produced. At the same time the habit of using judgment is weakened by the habit of depending on external stimuli. Upon the whole it is probably a tribute to the powers of endurance of human nature that the consequences are not more serious than they are.

The new mechanisms resulting from application of scientific discoveries have, of course, immensely extended the range and variety of particular events, or "news items" which are brought to bear upon the senses and the emotions connected with them. The telegraph, telephone, and radio report events going on over the whole face of the globe. They are for the most part events about which the individuals who are told of them can do nothing, except to react with a passing emotional excitation. For, because of lack of relation and organization in reference to one another, no imaginative reproduction of the situation is possible, such as might make up for the absence of personal response. Before we engage in too much pity for the inhabitants of our rural regions before the days of invention of modern devices for circulation of information, we should recall that they knew more about the things that affected their own lives than the city dweller of today is likely to know about the causes of his affairs. They did not possess nearly as many separate items of information, but they were compelled to know, in the sense of *understanding,* the conditions that bore upon the conduct of their own affairs. Today the influences that affect the actions performed by individuals are so remote as to be unknown. We are at the mercy of events acting upon us in unexpected, abrupt, and violent ways.

The bearing of these considerations upon the cultural conditions involved in maintenance of freedom is not far to seek. It is very directly connected with what now seems to us the oversimplification of the democratic idea indulged in by the authors of our republican government. They had in mind persons whose daily occupations stimulated initiative and vigor, and who possessed information which even if narrow in scope, bore pretty directly upon what they had to do, while its sources were pretty much within their control. Their judgment was exercised upon things within the range of their activities and their contacts. The press, the telegraph, the telephone and radio have broadened indefinitely the range of information at the disposal of the average person. It would be foolish to deny that a certain quickening of sluggish minds has resulted. But quite aside from having opened avenues through which organized propaganda may operate continuously to stir emotion and to leave behind a deposit of opinion, there is much information about which judgment is not called upon to respond, and where even if it wanted to, it cannot act effectively so dispersive is the material about which it is called upon to exert itself. The average person is surrounded today by readymade intellectual goods as he is by readymade foods, articles, and all kinds of gadgets. He has not the personal share in making either intellectual or material goods that his pioneer ancestors had. Consequently they knew better what they themselves were about, though they knew infinitely less concerning what the world at large was doing.

Self-government of the town-meeting type is adequate for management of local affairs, such as school buildings, district revenues, local roads and local taxation. Participation in these forms of self-government was a good preparation for self-government on a larger scale. But such matters as roads and schools under existing conditions have more than local import even in country districts; and while participation in town meetings is good as far as it arouses public spirit, it cannot provide the information that enables a citizen to be an intelligent judge of national affairs— now also affected by world conditions. Schooling in literacy is no substitute for the dispositions which were formerly provided by direct experiences of an educative quality. The void created by lack of relevant personal experiences combines with the confusion produced by impact of multitudes of unrelated incidents to create attitudes which are responsive to organized propaganda, hammering in day after day the same few and relatively simple beliefs asseverated to be "truths" essential to national welfare. In short, we have to take into account the attitudes of human nature that have been created by the immense development in mechanical instrumentalities if we are to understand the present power of organized propaganda.

The effect of the increase in number and diversity of unrelated facts that now play pretty continuously upon the average person is more easily grasped than is the influence of popular generalities, not checked by observed facts, over the interpretation put upon practical events, one that provokes acquiescence rather than critical inquiry. One chief reason for underestimation of the influence of generalities or "principles" is that they are so embodied in habits that those actuated by them are hardly aware of their existence. Or, if they are aware of them, they take them to be self-evident truths of common sense. When habits are so ingrained as to be second nature, they seem to have all of the inevitability that belongs to the movement of the fixed stars. The "principles" and standards which are stated in words and which circulate widely at a given time are usually only formulations of things which men do not so much believe in the intellectual sense of belief as live by unconsciously. Then when men who have lived under different conditions and have formed different life habits put forth different "principles," the latter are rejected as sources of some contagion introduced by foreigners hostile to our institutions.

Opinions are at once the most superficial and the most steel-plated of all human affairs. This difference between them is due to connection or lack of connection with habits that operate all but unconsciously. Verbal habits also exist and have power. Men continue to give assent to formulae after they have ceased to be more than linguistic rituals. Even lip-service has practical effect, that of creating intellectual and emotional divisions. The latter may not be deliberate hypocrisy. But they constitute that kind of insincerity, that incompatibility of actions with professions, which startles us in those cases in which it is clear that a person "believes" what he says in the sense that he is not even aware of its inconsistency with what he does. These gaps, these insincerities, become deeper and wider in times like the present when great change in events and practical affairs is attended with marked cultural lags in verbal formulations. And the persons who have first deceived themselves are most effective in misleading others. One of the most perplexing of human phenomena is the case of persons who do "in good faith" the sort of things which logical demonstration can easily prove to be incompatible with good faith.

Insincerities of this sort are much more frequent than deliberate hypocrisies and more injurious. They exist on a wide scale when there has been a period of rapid change in environment accompanied by change in what men do in response and by a change in overt habits, but without corresponding readjustment of the basic emotional and moral attitudes formed in the period prior to change of environment. This "cultural lag" is everywhere in evidence at the present time. The rate of change in conditions has been so much greater than anything the world has known before that it is estimated that the last century has seen more changes in the conditions under which people live and associate than occurred in thousands of previous years. The pace has been so swift that it was practically impossible for underlying traditions and beliefs to keep step. Not merely individuals here and there but large numbers of people habitually respond to conditions about them by means of actions having no connection with their familiar verbal responses. And yet the latter express dispositions saturated with emotions that find an outlet in words but not in acts.

No estimate of the effects of culture upon the elements that now make up freedom begins to be adequate that does not take into account the moral and religious splits that are found in our very make-up as persons. The problem of creation of genuine democracy cannot be successfully dealt with in theory or in practice save as we create intellectual and moral integration out of present disordered conditions. Splits, divisions, between attitudes emotionally and congenially attuned to the past and habits that are forced into existence because of the necessity of dealing with present conditions are a chief cause of continued profession of devotion to democracy by those who do not think nor act day by day in accord with the moral demands of the profession. The consequence is a further weakening of the environing conditions upon which genuine democracy occurs, whether the division is found in business men, in clergymen, in educators or in politicians. The serious threat to our democracy is not the existence of foreign totalitarian states. It is the existence within our own personal attitudes and within our own institutions of conditions similar to those which have given a victory to external authority, discipline, uniformity and dependence upon The Leader in foreign countries. The battlefield is also accordingly here—within ourselves and our institutions.

3. The American Background

While the sudden appearance of dictatorships and totalitarian states in Europe has raised such questions as have been asked, events in our country have put similar questions directly to ourselves. There is now raised the question of what was actually back of the formulation of the democratic faith a century and a half ago. Historians of the events that led up to the Declaration of Independence, the creation of the Confederation, and the adoption of the Federal Constitution tell us that what actually moved the leaders of the Rebellion against Great Britain were specific restrictions placed on industry and trade, together with levying of obnoxious taxes; and that what figured in doctrinal formulation as limitations upon inherent rights to freedom were in fact burdens imposed upon industrial pursuits from which persons of prestige and influence suffered economic losses.

Historians do not draw from their report of the concrete conditions, which, according to them, brought about the Revolution, the cynical conclusion that the ideas put forth about freedom, self-government and republican institutions were deliberate insincerities, intended to gull those who might otherwise have been indifferent in the struggle. It was rather that leaders generalized the particular restrictions from which they suffered into the general idea of oppression; and in similar fashion extended their efforts to get liberation from specific troubles into a struggle for liberty as a single all-embracing political ideal. The distance, the physical distance, between American settlers and British officials was so generalized that it became a symbol of the idea that all government not self-imposed is foreign to human nature and to human rights. In the language of modern psychology, a local struggle of a group to obtain release from certain specific abuses was "rationalized" into a universal struggle of humanity to obtain freedom in the abstract; a rationalization which, like other idealizations springing up in times of crisis, enabled men better to endure hardship and summon up energy for a struggle continued long enough to get rid of immediate abuses. They do not, as historians, draw the inference that anything that goes by the name of an active love for liberty is in fact but an effort to get liberation from some specific evil; and that when that evil is got rid of, men turn from love of liberty to enjoyment of the specific goods they happen to possess. But their account of facts suggests a conclusion of this sort.

Nor have these historians drawn the conclusion that economic forces are the only forces that move men to collective action, and that the state of forces of production is the ultimate factor in determining social relations. Historians have not ventured so far afield into broad generalizations. But in their capacity as historians they have pointed out the effect of specific economic factors in producing the Revolution; and of changed economic conditions, after the confusion of the period of the Confederation, in producing special provisions of the Constitution. They have called attention to the enduring influence upon political events of conflict of interests between farmers and traders. They show, for example, that the difference in the policies advocated by the Republican and Federal parties respectively during the first thirty or forty years of the Republic represent a difference in the interests of agricultural and commercial sections and groups: conflicts reflected in the party attitudes toward centralized and decentralized government, the power of the judiciary, especially of the supreme court, free trade and protective tariff, foreign policies with regard to France and Great Britain, etc.

The striking differences in temper between the Declaration of Independence and the Constitution are cited. That the first should be much the more radical in tone is easily explicable by the fact that it was written by the man who was the firmest and most explicit of all the leaders of the movement in faith in democracy. Conditions conspired to make him the spokesman at this juncture as changed conditions brought others to the front in the Constitutional Convention while he was absent in France. In one case, it was necessary to rally all the forces in the country in the name of freedom against a foreign foe. In the other case, the most urgent need of men of established position seemed

to be protection of established economic interests against on-
slaughts of a populace using liberty as a cloak for an attack upon
order and stability. There was also need of compromise to unite
various sections in a single federal government. Even during his
own lifetime the author of the Declaration of Independence
feared lest monarchical and oligarchical tendencies should undermine republic institutions.

Marxist social philosophy has made a sweeping generalization
where historians have been content to point out specific economic conditions operating in specific emergencies. The Marxist
has laid down a generalization that is supposed to state the law
governing the movement and final outcome of all the social
changes with which historians are occupied in detail. The generalization to which historians have pointed is rather a practical
maxim: If you wish to secure a certain political result, you must
see to it that economic conditions are such as to tend to produce
that result. If you wish to establish and maintain political self-
government, you must see to it that conditions in industry and
finance are not such as to militate automatically against your political aim.

This position leaves room for a great variety of shades of political opinion and practical policies, all the way from political action to curb tendencies toward monopolies when the latter gain
undue strength to attempts to "socialize" industry and finance.
The Marxist position, on the other hand, lays down a universal
law claimed to be scientific. It derives its practical policies from
adherence, actual or alleged, to the "law" which is formulated.

Whether the effect of the economic factor upon political conditions is taken in its moderate or its extreme form, the facts involved tremendously complicate the problem of democratic freedom as it existed when the Union was formed. The original
democratic theory was simple in its formulation because the conditions under which it took effect were simple. As theory, it
postulated a widespread desire in human nature for personal
freedom, for release from dominion over personal beliefs and
conduct that is exercised from sources external to the individual.
Combined with belief in this desire was the belief, generated by
the conditions that had provoked the struggle for independence,
that the chief enemy to realization of the desire was the tendency

of government officials to extend their power without limit. Guarantees against this abuse were then supposed to be enough to establish republican government.

The latter belief was a manifestation of the existing struggle to obtain independence from British rule. It was strengthened by memories of conditions which had induced many persons to emigrate from the old country. In the case of Jefferson, the most intellectual and the most definitely explicit of all the American leaders, it was strengthened by what he personally observed during his residence in France. What he experienced there led him to give unqualified support to the saying that in a country with an oppressive government everyone is either hammer or anvil. The doctrine received negative support, if I may put the matter in that way, from the fact that there was in the late eighteenth century no other organized foe to freedom visible above the horizon—although Jefferson anticipated with dread the rise of such an enemy in the growth of manufacturing and commerce and the growth of cities of large populations.

In any event, the heart of the doctrine as a theory was a virtual identification of freedom with the very state of being an individual; and the extent of freedom that existed was taken to be the measure of the degree in which individuality was realized. It is possible to interpret this attitude and faith in two different ways. According to one view, it was an expression of pioneer conditions; it was appropriate to those conditions but was thoroughly naïve as a universal truth about the individual and about government. According to the other view, while the idea had some of the qualities of a dream, yet it expresses a principle to be maintained by deliberative effort if mankind is to have a truly human career. Call it dream or call it vision, it has been interwoven in a tradition that has had an immense effect upon American life.

However, the influence of tradition is two-fold. On the one hand, it leads to effort to perpetuate and strengthen the conditions which brought it into existence. But, on the other hand, a tradition may result in habits that obstruct observation of what is actually going on; a mirage may be created in which republican institutions are seen as if they were in full vigor after they have gone into a decline. There are now persons who think that the anti-democratic effect of economic development has so far destroyed essential democracy that only by the democratization or "socialization" of industry and finance can political democracy be restored. Whatever be thought of this view, its existence marks an immense change in conditions. To the Founding Fathers control of production and distribution of commodities and services by means of any political agency whatsoever would have seemed the complete nullification of all they were fighting for. A similar belief is still put forward with especial strength when a movement, even a moderate one, is made toward social control of business by political action—which is then denounced as the destruction of "Americanism." No matter which side (if either) is right, the division is not helpful to the democratic cause.

We are not concerned to decide which one of the different schools of social theory is correct. We are not even concerned at this point to judge whether governmental action is necessarily hostile to the maintenance of personal freedom or whether the latter becomes an empty shell if it is without organized political backing. The point is the complication of the earlier situation regarding freedom which is made evident when it is possible for men to urge that preservation of democratic institutions requires just that extension of governmental functions which to the authors of our tradition was the enemy to be fought. Whatever school of social philosophy be right, the situation has been transformed since the day when the problem of freedom and democracy presented itself as essentially a *personal* problem capable of being decided by strictly personal choice and action. For, according to the earlier idea, about all that was needed was to keep alive a desire for freedom, which is inherent in the very constitution of individuals, and jealously to watch the actions of governmental officials. Given these basic conditions, the means required for perpetuation of self-government were simple. They were exhausted in personal responsibility of officials to the citizens for whom they are but delegates; general suffrage; frequent elections so that officials would have to give frequent accounts of the way they had used their powers; majority rule; and keeping the units of government as small as possible so that people would know what their representatives were up to. These measures, combined with complete abolition of whatever traces of the feudal system had been brought over from England, were sufficient, provided only a Bill of Rights was adopted and kept in force. For the Bill of Rights gave guarantees against certain specific encroachments of governmental officials upon personal freedom—such as arbitrary arrest. It instituted the moral and psychological conditions of self-government by securing the rights of free speech, free press, free assembly, free choice of creed. Given the maintenance of these rights, the few and simple governmental mechanisms mentioned would make secure the cause of free institutions.

That the conditions which influence the working of governmental mechanisms and the maintenance of the liberties constituting the Bill of Rights are infinitely more complex than they were a century and a half ago is evident beyond need for argument. Whether one is a believer in the necessity for increased social control of economic activities or in allowing the maximum possible of private initiative in industry and exchange, both sides must admit that impersonal forces have been set in motion on a scale undreamed of in the early days of the Republic.

Whatever else is reasonably settled or is unsettled, it is certain that the ratio of impersonal to personal activities in determining the course of events has enormously increased. The machine as compared with the hand tool is an impersonal agency. Free land and an abundance of unappropriated and unused natural resources—things which brought men in face-to-face personal connection with Nature and which also kept individual persons in pretty close contact with one another—have been replaced by impersonal forces working on a vast scale, with causes and effects so remote as not to be perceptible. A symbolic example is the change in production between the day when a comparatively small number of "hired hands" worked side by side with their employer in a shop, and modern factories with hundreds or thousands of laborers who never see the owners (who moreover, as scattered shareholders, do not even know one another); and who come in contact with those immediately responsible for the conduct of the work only through delegates. Need for large capital to carry on mass production has also separated even personal financial liability from ownership. The whole significance of property has changed. "Private" property, in its old sense, has disappeared. Or, if another illustration is needed, there is the replacement of village life where everyone knew everybody else's character by congested cities in which persons do not know the persons who live on the same floor with them; and where, on the political side, they are called upon to vote for a large number of persons many of whom they cannot identify even by name.

The point is the intervention of an indefinite number of indefinitely ramifying conditions between what a person does and the consequences of his actions, including even the consequences which return upon him. The intervals in time and space are so extensive that the larger number of factors that decide the final outcome cannot be foreseen. Even when they can be anticipated, the results are produced by factors over which the average person has hardly any more control than he has over those which produce earthquakes. The recurrence of large-scale unemployment with sharp curtailment of production and the consequent instability of the conditions of both employer and employed is a convincing example. When all allowance is made for shiftlessness and incompetency of employees and for recklessness on the part of the employer, the recurrence of these crises cannot be understood save as evidence of the working of forces operating beyond the possibility of personal control. The current proposal to take away the vote from persons on relief, if it were supplemented by a proposal to deprive of suffrage all employers who are not paying their debts, would carry out the Biblical remark about taking away from those who have not even that which they seem to have.

When conditions that make for unemployment are as extensively ramified as they are at present, political action assumes an importance for workers, employed and unemployed, that it does not have when conditions are settled and opportunity for employment is fairly general and secure. There are movements in all industrialized countries to provide work by governmental projects; there are schemes for offsetting, by doles and official relief, evils that have resulted from the failure of industrialists and financial captains to provide the means of livelihood. The chiefly palliative nature of these measures is an evidence that symptoms rather than causes are dealt with; and this fact is in turn further proof that fundamental economic conditions are so far out of control that emergency measures are resorted to. The fact that evils are not remedied and in some respects are aggravated calls out a reaction in favor of return to individual initiative—that is, leaving the course of events to determination by those who have a store of resources in reserve.

There is little to prevent this reaction from making temporary headway. For the chief phenomenon in American politics at the present time is that voters are moved primarily by the ills which are easily seen to be those from which they and the country at large are suffering. Since the evils are attributed more or less to the action of the party in power, there is a succession of swings back and forward as the relative impotency of this and that party and of this and that line of policy to regulate economic conditions, sufficiently to prevent widespread disaster, becomes clear. This impotency of existing political forms to direct the working and the social effects of modern industry has operated to generate distrust of the working of parliamentary institutions and all forms of popular government. It explains why democracy is now under attack from both the right and the left. There is no reason to suppose that a country as highly industrialized as the United States is immune.

While the possessing class is relatively more secure, yet its members are also profoundly unsettled by recurring cyclic depression. Emergence in political life of populist movements, square deals, new deals, accompanies depressions on the part of those most directly affected—farmers, factory laborers, etc., who are kept from uniting politically by divergence of immediate interests. But it would be foolish to suppose that the well-to-do class, the class of employers and investors, is not unsettled in a way that stirs it to political action to strengthen its hold on the agencies of political action. As the activities increase of the groups which are radical from the standpoint of the possessing class, and especially as they fail to effect a fundamental remedy of the situation, the activities of the favored economic class increase. When disorders appear on any considerable scale, the adherence of the middle class to the side of "law and order" is won. Ironically enough, the desire for security which proceeds from the two groups of very different economic status combines to increase readiness to surrender democratic forms of action. The coalescence of desire for security from two opposite sources has been a factor in the substitution of dictators for parliaments in European countries. The danger of the rise of an American Fascist movement in this country comes from a similar source. It is absurd to suppose that the class having relatively the superior economic status can promote a dictatorship unless it has strong popular support—which means the support of those relatively at a disadvantage. "Security" is a word covering a great diversity of interests, and all of them have a bearing upon the conditions required for maintenance of democracy.

In brief, economic developments which could not possibly have been anticipated when our political forms took shape have created confusion and uncertainty in the working of the agencies of popular government, and thereby have subjected the idea of democracy to basic strain. The change in conditions goes far beyond the particular consequences which Jefferson feared as a result of growth of manufacturing and trade at the expense of agriculture. The strengthening of the political power of laborers that occurred in Great Britain as the consequence of industrialization, and the part played by this factor in the liberalization of government, were not anticipated by him. In so far, there is no special cause for surprise in the fact that the interests originally represented by Jefferson and Hamilton have now changed places with respect to exercise of federal political power. For Jeffersonian principles of self-government, of the prime authority of the people, of general happiness or welfare as the end of government, can be appealed to in support of policies that are opposite to those urged by Jefferson in his day.

The real problem is deeper. There is no well-defined continuity of political movement because of the confusion that exists in general social movements. That the general trend is toward increase of public control of private industry and finance in the United States as in other countries is undeniable. But the movement is not clear-cut in theory nor are its consequences consistent in practice. In fact, there is one thesis of Herbert Spencer that could now be revived with a good deal of evidence in its support: namely, the economic situation is so complex, so intricate in the interdependence of delicately balanced factors, that planned policies initiated by public authority are sure to have consequences totally unforeseeable,—often the contrary of what was intended—as has happened in this country rather notably in connection with some of the measures undertaken for control of agricultural production.

So far I have been speaking of the fairly direct impact of economic conditions upon democratic political habits and beliefs. The mining and sapping have not begun to go so far in this country as in European countries which have adopted some form of National Socialism. But uncertainty and confusion and increasing scepticism about the relevancy of political democracy to present conditions, have been created. In this connection another effect of change from conditions which relatively were capable of being seen and regulated by personal skill and personal insight must be noted. The comparative helplessness of persons in their strictly singular capacities to influence the course of events expresses itself in formation of combinations in order to secure protection from too destructive impact of impersonal forces. That groups now occupy much the same place that was occupied earlier by individuals is almost a commonplace of writers on sociology. For example, trades unions for collective bargaining in regulation of wages, hours and physical conditions of work are produced on one side; pools, mergers, syndicates, trusts and employers' associations, often with command of armed strikebreakers, are generated on the other side. The theory of the self-actuated and self-governing individual receives a rude shock when massed activity has a potency which individual effort can no longer claim.

The growth of organized combinations has had an effect on that part of democratic doctrine which held that all men should be free as well as equal. The doctrine of equality never meant what some of its critics supposed it to mean. It never asserted equality of natural gifts. It was a moral, a political and legal principle, not a psychological one. Thomas Jefferson believed as truly in a "natural aristocracy" as did John Adams. The existence of marked psychological inequalities was indeed one of the reasons why it was considered so important to establish political and legal equality. For otherwise those of superior endowment might, whether intentionally or without deliberation, reduce those of inferior capacity to a condition of virtual servitude. The words "nature" and "natural" are among the most ambiguous of all the words used to justify courses of action. Their very ambiguity is one source of their use in defense of any measure and end regarded as desirable. The words mean what is native, what is original or innate, what exists at birth in distinction from what is acquired by cultivation and as a consequence of experience. But it also means that which men have got used to, inured to by custom, that imagination can hardly conceive of anything different. Habit is second nature and second nature under ordinary circumstances as potent and urgent as first nature. Again, nature has a definitely moral import; that which is *normal* and hence is right; that which should be.

The assertion that men are free and equal by nature unconsciously, possibly deliberately, took advantage of the prestige possessed by what is "natural" in the first two senses to reinforce the moral force of the word. That "naturalness" in the moral sense provided the imperative ethical foundation of politics and law was, however, the axiomatic premise of democratic theory. Exercise of a liberty which was taken to be a moral right has in the course of events, especially economic events, seriously threatened the moral right to legal and political equality. While we may not believe that the revolutionary effect of steam, electricity, etc., has nullified moral faith in equality, their operation has produced a new difficult problem. The effect of statutes, of administrative measures, of judicial decisions, upon the maintenance of equality and freedom cannot be estimated in terms of fairly direct personal consequences. We have first to estimate their effects upon complicated social conditions (largely a matter of guesswork), and then speculate what will be the effect of the new social conditions upon individual persons.

Even if everybody, no matter how unequal in other endowments, possessed in like measure the faculty of reason or of common sense with which the optimistic rationalism of the eighteenth century supposed men to be equipped, the faculty would not go far in judging causes and effects of political and legal action at the present time. What purports to be experiment in the social field is very different from experiment in natural science; it is rather a process of trial and error accompanied with some degree of hope and a great deal of talk. Legislation is a matter of more or less intelligent improvisation aiming at palliating conditions by means of patchwork policies. The apparent alternative seems to be a concentration of power that points toward ultimate dictatorship. Since at best legislation can only pass measures in general terms, which are not self-interpreting much less self-applying, and since it is a costly and uncertain process to wait upon decisions of the courts to ascertain what laws mean in the concrete, administrative bodies possessed of large powers are multiplied—in spite of their inconsistency with the doctrine of the three-fold division of powers that is still the nominal constitutional theory. Persons of a liberal outlook, captured by fear of dictatorship, join with persons whose special and anti-social interests are unfavorably affected by the action of these commissions and indulge in wholesale attack—failing to see that new administrative bodies are so imperatively needed that the real problem is that of building up an intelligent and capable civil-service under conditions that will operate against formation of rigid bureaucracies.

The point which is here pertinent is that early theory and practice assumed an inherent, and so to say pre-established, harmony between liberty and equality. As liberty has been practiced in industry and trade, the economic inequalities produced have reacted against the existence of equality of opportunity. Only those who have a special cause to plead will hold that even in the most democratic countries, under the most favorable conditions, have children of the poor the same chances as those of the well-to-do, even in a thing like schooling which is supported at public expense. And it is no consoling offset that the children of the rich often suffer because of the one-sided conditions under which they grow up.

The way in which the problem of the relation of liberty and equality was earlier conceived is perhaps most clearly exhibited in the pains taken in the French Revolution to prevent combinations and associations from growing up, even those of a voluntary sort; so convinced were the leaders of the revolutionary doctrine of Liberty, Equality and Fraternity that combinations are hostile to liberty. The laws against trade unions as conspiracies, which existed in England, had a very different source. But fear of combination and organization from whatever source it has emanated, liberal or reactionary, gives evidence of the existence of a problem. Even the late President Eliot voiced a not uncommon belief of a certain type of liberal in his jealous fear lest the growth of labor unions put restrictions upon the liberty of wage-earners to work when and where and how they individually liked, an attitude that still appears on a large scale when it is a question of the closed shop. Persons who are favorable "in principle" to collective bargaining shrink when the principle is systematically applied. Once more the point here pertinent is not who is right and who is wrong, but the fact that the conditions of industry and commerce produced by existing technologies have created in a wholly unanticipated way the problem of the relation of organization and freedom—with what philosophers call an antinomy as a result.

For there are convincing arguments both that individuals can be free only in connection with large-scale organizations and that such organizations are limitations of freedom. In any case, the organized associations of wage-workers in labor unions and of capitalistic employers in pools, combines, mergers, trusts, syndicates, gentlemen's agreements, are two aspects of the same process; while that indefinite amorphous thing called the consuming public tends by turns to be about equally suspicious of both, according to which one seems most active at a given time in producing a visible inconvenience. Just how mass-production and mass-distribution together with elimination of spatial barriers by speedy transportation and communication could have come into existence without consolidation and concentration on a large scale it is impossible to explain. And yet many who adhere to the letter rather than to the spirit of the early formulation of democratic faith will be found deploring or denouncing one or the other of the two forms of organizations that had come into existence as destructive of the ideals of liberty and equality—a fact which proves that a new type of problem has come into existence, whatever be its solution.

Growing distrust of the efficacy of parliamentary bodies is, as has been intimated, a result of the increased complexity of events. How can a collection of men, selected chiefly upon grounds of party availability, have either the knowledge or the skill required to cope with such extensive interlocking conditions as now exist? Some measure of conflict between the legislative body and the executive is an old story in American life whenever the President has happened to have strong convictions of his own; and it is a fact of a wider history than the American that in the case of such a conflict the executive tends to set himself up as an agent of the masses and the legislative body to be so selected as to be close to special interests. Difficulties in the way of effective action by law-making bodies in meeting actual conditions are increased by the general belief that they, with the courts and with administrative bodies, are favorable to special interests, by association and by education and at times by corruption. Distrust gives both the rabble-rouser and the would-be dictator their opportunities. The former speaks in words for the oppressed mass against oppression; in historic fact he has usually been an agent, willing or unknowing, of a new form of oppression. As Huey Long is reported to have said, Fascism would come in this country under the name of protecting democracy from its enemies.

Any adequate discussion of the present relations of politics and economics would have to extend to conditions in village, city, county, state and nation, and its conclusions would fill volumes. Its conclusions would enforce in detail the thesis that the interconnections and interdependence of industry and government puts a radically new face upon the problem of democratic policies. I shall mention but one more fact of those that could be cited. Modern industry could not have reached its present development without legalization of the corporation. The corporation is a creature of the state: that is, of political action. It has no existence save by the action of legislatures and courts. Many of the earlier arguments for limitation and extreme decentralization of political power were virtually outlawed when the first statute authorizing the formation of business corporations was passed. The bitter struggle in this country between business interests and governmental actions has been in large degree a struggle to see whether the child begot by the state or the progenitor should control the subsequent activities of the parent. Operation of the state-created corporation under the decisions of the courts is proof positive that the careers of politics and business cross and mix in intimate and manifold ways, all of them unforeseeable when our governmental arrangements took shape. Epigrams about the difference between the day of the stagecoach and of the railway and airplane are at best only suggestions of the enormous change in human relationships that has been produced by change in the means by which industry is carried on. The new relations require a new determination of rights and duties. The determination of them made during the time when the chief problem was that of maintaining peaceful relations between persons as persons is not adequate to determine rights and obligations when large combinations have largely replaced individual persons as the units of effective action. The very necessity for change only makes urgent the question of whether the existing agencies of democracy are competent to effect the change.

This is the basic question pointed to by the considerations which have been barely sketched. It is the problem which has precedence over the various plans and policies that are urged from one quarter or another. Consider, as an example, the argument that since the *processes* of industry, on the side of both labor and capital, have become collective, ownership and control must also be collective, resulting in elimination of private income from rent, interest and dividends. From the standpoint of democracy, this end, which is put forward in the interest of maintenance of democracy, raises the problem of the possibility of its execution by democratic methods. Can the change be effected by democratic means? After it is effected, supposing that it is, can production and distribution of goods and services be effected except by a centralized power that is destructive of democracy? The first of these two questions finds a profound split existing among professed socialists. Some of them hold the transition can be effected by recognized democratic means. But a larger and at present more vigorous section holds that democratic states are inherently bound up with just the things to be eliminated. Hence it is absurd—or, worse, deliberate deception—to believe the change can be effected by any means save violent overthrow of existing political governments and transfer of power to representatives of workers, urban factory workers at that. According to this view, the political state always has been and by its very nature is an arm of the dominant political class, and as long as that class is bourgeois capitalism, it is axiomatic with them that change must proceed from its complete overthrow.

Suppose the great change has come about, whether by one procedure or the other, what then? Asking the question is almost equivalent to calling attention to the relatively slight attention the underlying issue has received. For the most part the answer is to the effect that sufficient to the day is the evil or the good thereof. Since it would be utopian to try to imagine the details of a social state such as has never existed, energies should be taken up either with bringing about the violent revolution or with the educative process required for a peaceful transition to a socialist society. Many socialists of the latter type remain within our democratic tradition in believing that the continued use of democratic methods will mature those methods so that they will be effective in dealing with special problems as the latter arise. Nevertheless, the fact that popular ideas about socialism identify it with state or government socialism, while democratic socialists are strongly opposed to the latter—unless perhaps as a transitional stage—shows that the problem has not had a great deal of attention, syndicalist socialists being the faction that has considered it most explicitly.

So far social control of industry has mostly taken the form of regulation or ownership exercised under governmental auspices by governmental officials. This is so in National Socialist, in Bolshevist Socialist countries, and in democratic countries. Neither theory nor practical experience has as yet shown that state socialism will be essentially different from state capitalism. Even if we are obliged to abandon permanently the earlier belief that governmental action is by its own momentum hostile to free self-government, we are far from having refuted the evidence of history that officials who have political power will use it arbitrarily. Belief in what is sometimes called taking industry out of private hands is naïve until it is shown that the new private—or personal—hands to which it is confided are so controlled that they are reasonably sure to work in behalf of public ends. I am not saying the problem cannot be solved democratically nor that "socialization" of industry is bound to be followed by the regimentation so freely predicted by adherents of *laissez-faire* individualism. What I am saying is that the issue of democracy has taken a new form, where not much experience is available about the relation of economic factors, as they now operate, to democratic ends and methods.

In the absence of adequate experience, the tendency is to set up wholesale theories in opposition to one another; the current statement of the human problem as individualism versus socialism being both a reflex expression of the divisions in the economic factors of present society, and an example of wholesale opposition. In such an opposition of ideas, each theory thrives on the weaknesses of the other one; confusion is thereby increased. If it is utopian to expect a new social order will be ushered in as soon as industry is "socialized"—with little idea of what that means save negatively, or abolition of private profit, interest, rent and returns from fixed investment—it is highly unrealistic to go on repeating phrases about the connection of industry with personal independence, initiative and other desirable qualities that had a meaning in agrarian pioneer conditions. The idea of a pre-established harmony between the existing so-called capitalistic regime and democracy is as absurd a piece of metaphysical speculation as human history has ever evolved.

The strife of interests, parties and factions is especially harmful since the problem is a common human one, the ways in which it is dealt with and their results affecting all alike. The first necessity is study of the scientifically cooperative type. It is theoretically conceivable that strife of interests might bring to clearer recognition the different interests that are involved and that have to be harmonized in any enduring solution. As long, however, as conflict is conducted on the assumption, upon each side, that there is already possession of the truth, a position that amounts to denial for the need of any scientific examination of conditions in order to determine the policies that should be undertaken, the rivalry of parties will be a source of division and confusion.

The discussion of this chapter has been one-sided in its emphasis upon the economic phase of our culture. But industrialization and commercialization play such a part in determining the qualities of present culture that the primary need for analysis of its conditions is made especially clear. The facts that justify economic emphasis do not prove, however, that the issue of cooperative democratic freedom can be settled by dealing directly and exclusively with the economic aspect, if only because command of the means which would be needed to effect desirable changes in industry and in the distribution of income can be achieved only by the aid of correlative changes in science, morals and other phases of our common experience. The facts bring out in sharp outline that as yet the full conditions, economic and legal, for a completely democratic experience have not existed. Upon both the negative and the positive side, the facts suggest the importance of critical examination of the theory that attaches supremacy to economic factors in isolation. The significance of interaction will appear more clearly in the contrast.

4. Totalitarian Economics and Democracy

Social movements that have a new direction are accompanied by simplifications. Imagination ignores things that might obscure singleness of vision; plans ignore whatever gets in the way of concentrated energy. Later on, the things that were left out of the reckoning are noted. They are then seen to be involved in the failure to realize the original program. Disappointment and frustration succeed a period of enthusiasms; hope is followed by sober and critical second thought. There is often discouragement as to the practical value of any large social outlook. What is thought to be hard realism and is certainly an emotional disillusionment comes after a period of romantic idealism. We were in that state to a considerable degree until the rise of totalitarian states issued a challenge that compels us to reconsider fundamental principles.

It is easy to overlook later advantages that were obtained by an earlier simplification. Benefits wrought and harm done are wrongly located both at the time of origin and of later criticism. Simplification is beneficial as far as it brings about clear recognition of some new operative tendency in human affairs, a fuller and freer operation of which would occasion enrichment of human life. The exaggeration tends to make the new factor stand out in relief; acknowledgment of it then becomes a positive influence in furthering it, so that it works deliberately instead of more or less unconsciously. Harm comes from the fact that the theory framed is stated in absolute terms, as one which applies at all places and times, instead of under the contemporary conditions and having definite limits. Later, when conditions have undergone such a change that the idea does not work, a reaction sets in which is equally wholesale. The original idea is dismissed as pure illusion; some newer movement, going contrary to the conditions which evoked the earlier idea, is then often given similar absoluteness.

pendulum

62

Since the rise of natural science and its attendant technologies, simplifications on the side of theory have been of two general classes. Theories have simplified in exaggeration of either the human factor, the constituents derived from human nature, or the "external" environing factor. Popular ideas are usually a more or less confused and inconsistent compromise, drawing some elements from each point of view and combining them in a haphazard way. Clarification may, then, be had if in this chapter and the next, we consider two types of theory that carry one-sided simplifications to extremes, extremes which are logical, given the premises, but which mislead action because of the absolute quality of the premises. The kind of theory thus formed contrasts radically with the procedure in which social events are seen to be *interactions* of components of human nature on one side with cultural conditions on the other. Events are explained as if one factor or other in the interaction were the whole thing. In this chapter, I shall criticize the type of social theory which reduces the human factor as nearly as possible to zero; since it explains events and frames policies exclusively in terms of conditions provided by the environment. Marxism is taken as the typical illustration of the absolutism which results when this factor in the interaction is isolated and made supreme. It provides a typical illustration both because of its present vogue, and because it claims to represent the only strictly scientific theory of social change and thereby the method by which to effect change in the future.

Since the theory is involved in practical and party controversies in which feelings are excited, it is almost useless to say that the theory is here discussed as an illustration of what may be called "objective" or "realistic" absolutism, and for the sake of the light which thereby is thrown upon the actual problems of the present. For its adherents, by reason of the very nature of the theory, readily become so absolutistic in their attitude that they can see only a display of class-bias, unconscious or deliberate, in any criticism of their theory—an attitude now summed up in calling any opposition pro-Fascist. With those not committed it may promote understanding if I say that the criticism is not aimed at denying the role of economic factors in society nor at denying the tendency of the present economic regime to produce consequences adverse to democratic freedom. These things are rather taken for granted. Criticism aims to show what happens when this undeniable factor is isolated and treated as *the* cause of *all* social change. One may hold that if there is to be genuine and adequate democracy there must be a radical transformation of the present controls of production and distribution of goods and services, and may nevertheless accept the criticisms to be made—indeed may make or accept the criticisms *because* one believes the transformation is required.

The Marxist isolation of one factor (one which actually operates only in interaction with another one) takes the form of holding that the state of the forces of economic productivity at a given time ultimately determines all forms of social activities and relations, political, legal, scientific, artistic, religious, moral. In its original formulation, there was an important qualification which later statements have tended to ignore. For it was admitted that when political relations, science, etc., are once produced, they operate as causes of subsequent events, and in this capacity are capable of modifying in some degree the operation of the forces which originally produced them.

The subsequent ignoring of this qualification, the relegation of it to a footnote, was not wholly accidental. For there were practical reasons for paying little attention to it. If the qualification be admitted, observation of existing conditions (not the theory in the abstract) can alone tell just what consequences at a given time are produced by secondary effects which have now themselves acquired the standing of causes. The only way to decide would be to investigate, and by investigation in the concrete decide just what effects are due, say, to science, and just what to the naked, so to say, forces of economic production. To adopt and pursue this method would be in effect to abandon the all-comprehensive character of economic determination. It would put us in the relativistic and pluralistic position of considering a number of interacting factors—of which a very important one is undoubtedly the economic.

Marx would have a distinguished historic position if the qualification were admitted in even fuller extent than he allowed for. He would not have been the first by any means to recognize the importance of economic conditions in determination of political and legal forms. Their close connection was almost a commonplace of the political philosophy of Aristotle. It was restated in a different form by English writers who influenced the ideas of the founders of the American republic. The latter uniformly emphasized connection between a certain state of the distribution of property and secure maintenance of popular government. But Marx did go back of property relations to the working of the forces of production as no one before him had done. He also discriminated between the state of the forces of product*ivity* and the actual state of production existing at a given time, pointing out the lag often found in the latter. He showed in considerable detail that the cause of the lag is subordination of productive forces to legal and political conditions holding over from a previous regime of production. Marx's criticism of the present state of affairs from this last point of view was penetrating and possessed of enduring value.

The great merit, however, of the Marxist simplification, for those who accept it in its extreme form, is the fact that it combines the romantic idealism of earlier social revolutionaries with what purports to be a thoroughly "objective" scientific analysis, expressed in formulation of a single all-embracing "law," a law which moreover sets forth the proper method to be followed by the oppressed economic class in achieving its final liberation. For the theory went far beyond presenting a point of view to be employed in historical and sociological investigations. It claimed to state the one and only law in accordance with which economic relations determine the course of social change. This law is that of the existence of classes which are economically determined, which are engaged in constant warfare with one another, the outcome of which is direction of social change toward the liberation of producers from the bonds which have kept them subjugated in the past. Final creation of a classless society is to be the outcome.

It is quite possible to accept the idea of some sort of economic determinism. But that acceptance does not constitute one a Marxian, since the essence of the latter is the view that class warfare is the channel through which economic forces operate to effect social change and progress. This "law" was not derived nor supposed to be derived from study of historical events. It was derived from Hegelian dialectical metaphysics. The method of its derivation is indicated by the saying of Marx that he stood Hegel on his head. Hegel's system is one of dialectic idealism, in which logical categories, through the movement inherent in any partial and incomplete formulation of the rational structure of the universe, generate their own opposites, while the union of these opposites constitutes a higher and more adequate grasp of the nature of things, until finally all possible points of view with all their seeming conflicts are "organic" constituents of one all-comprehensive system.

Marx converted dialectic idealism into dialectic material-ism—where the dialectic of conflict as the means of ultimate union and harmony is preserved, while the moving forces are economic classes, not ideas. Its "materialism" is therefore as dif-ferent from "vulgar" materialism, based solely on conclusions of physical science, as the ultimate socialism, or the final synthesis of classless society is different from the "utopian" socialism of earlier communists:—utopian because they gave power and im-petus to human preferences of values, thereby assigning causal power to moral factors. To Marx the economic movement is nec-essarily as self-determined toward its ultimate goal as the move-ment of logical categories had been in the Hegelian system. Marxism thus not only dropped the idealistic rationalism of the Hegelian system and violently condemned it, but he also, in the name of science, denied moving power to human valuations.

In lieu of one type of romantic absolutism, it developed another type more in harmony with the prestige which science and scien-tific law were gaining. It was a wonderful intellectual achievement to formulate laws for all social phenomena; it was still more wonderful to set forth one law working with absolute necessity, grasp of which enabled men to observe the "contradictions" in existing bourgeois capitalism, while it indicated with certainty the goal to which the contradictions by their own dialectic were carrying society. The law of history became the law for revolu-tionary action:—and all was accomplished that can possibly be accomplished in behalf of a clear vision of a goal and the con-centration of emotion and energy in its behalf.

The idea of causal necessity in social phenomena and of devel-opment or "evolution" were in the intellectual atmosphere a century ago, the latter anteceding the Darwinian notion of bio-logical development. Kant had taught that the idea of causal ne-cessity is a prerequisite for natural science; German scientists at least accepted the idea without question, especially as Kant also made a sharp division between the fields of science and that of morals where freedom reigned. Hume's criticism of the idea of necessity was unwelcome even when it was known, because of its association with scepticism. In any case Kant seemed to have made an adequate reply to Hume.

In almost every quarter attempts were made to create a science of social phenomena, for which undertaking the idea of necessary law was deemed indispensable. Auguste Comte introduced the word *Sociology* as a name for a comprehensive synthesis, while he found its basis in the "law" of three necessary stages of development. At a later period, Herbert Spencer had no difficulty in finding a single formula to cover all phenomena, cosmic, biological, psychological, social. The earlier attempts at introducing scientific arrangement into human events made use of the principle of stages of necessary "evolution" in some form or other.

The forties of the last century were also the time of promising radical political movements, all of which had a marked economic slant, while some were avowedly socialistic and communistic, especially at that time in France. There was a period in Germany when Hegel's philosophy was so dominant that all important differences were those between wings of the Hegelian school. All of these circumstances put together, it is not surprising that Marx saw in the Hegelian dialectic a principle which, when it was given economic interpretation, provided a sure basis for a science of social changes, while at the same time, it furnished the revolutionary movement a supreme directive for its practical activities.

As has been said, important social movements develop some sort of philosophy by which to guide, nominally, at least, their practical efforts and also to justify them *ex post facto*. German culture has been especially ardent and prolific in this direction, all attempts to deal with actual conditions on any other basis being regarded as proof that those engaged in them are mere "empiricists," a term of condemnation about equivalent to calling them quacks. In Marxism those who accepted any law except one having exclusively material support were utopian dreamers. The fact then that the dialectical formula was borrowed from the most metaphysical, in a non-scientific sense, of all modern philosophers was no deterrent to the vogue of the Marxist synthesis, since its practical character seemed to be vouched for not only by actual economic conditions and by Marx's predictions, but in particular by the increase in class conflict that was taking place.

The idea of class war took on a peculiarly timely quality because of its teaching that the then existing class struggle was that of bourgeoisie capitalists with the proletariat, the class of factory wage-workers having neither land nor any form of reserve capital. Moreover, Marx's study of the concrete facts of the factory system in Great Britain backed up his general theory with a considerable number of economic generalizations which proved sound on any theory:—such as the existence of economic cycles with crises of increasing severity, a tendency toward combination and concentration, etc. The simplified Romanticism of the principle of a negation of negations taught that class war would, through the mediation of a temporary dictatorship of the proletariat, finally usher in a classless society. In the latter the state as a political coercive power would wither away, all political agencies becoming organs of democratic administration of affairs of common interest. Even the anarchist with his opposition to all coercive power could find satisfaction in contemplation of this ultimate outcome.

Marxists object vigorously and naturally to any suggestion of an identification of their creed with theological systems of the past. But all absolutisms tend to assume a theological form and to arouse the kind of emotional ardor that has accompanied crusading religions in the past. The theological concerns and conflicts of the earlier centuries of our era involved, moreover, contemporary interests not now recoverable in imagination. That is, they were more "practical" in fact than they now appear in retrospect. Similarly the monolithic and in itself speculative Marxist doctrine took on immediate practical coloring in connection with existing economic conditions and new forms of oppressions they had produced. There is nothing novel or peculiar in a combination of theory and practice in which practical events give definite color to an abstract theory, while the theory serves as a fountainhead of inspiration to action, providing also rallying cries and slogans. Exegesis can always serve to bridge gaps and inconsistencies; and every absolutistic creed demonstrates that no limits can be put to exegetical ingenuity. What actually happens can, accordingly, be brought into harmony with dogma while the latter is covertly accommodated to events.

There is no need to go into the full scope of Marxist philosophy upon its theoretical side. What is of concern here is the support alleged to be given by it to a strictly *scientific* form of social development, one which is inevitable *because* scientific. As is said of literary products, Marxism is "dated" in the matter of its claims to be peculiarly scientific. For just as *necessity* and search for a *single* all-comprehensive law was typical of the intellectual atmosphere of the forties of the last century, so *probability* and *pluralism* are the characteristics of the present state of science. That the older interpretation of the idea of causal necessity has undergone a shock does not need to be told to those acquainted with recent developments. It is not necessary, however, to go to the point of throwing the idea entirely overboard to make the point which is significant for the present topic.

There is a worldwide difference between the idea that causal sequences will be found in any given set of events taken for investigation, and the idea that *all* sets of events are linked together into a *single* whole by *one* causal law. Even if it be admitted that the former principle is a necessary postulate of scientific inquiry, the latter notion is metaphysical and *extra*-scientific. When natural science was first struggling to achieve its independence, and later when an attempt was made to take social phenomena out of the domain of arbitrary free-will, those who wanted to promote the new struggles borrowed from dominant theology the idea which the latter had made familiar, that of a single all-embracing causal force. The nature of the force and the way it worked were radically altered in the new apologetics for science. But the requirements of habit were satisfied in maintaining the old forms of thought—just as the first "horseless carriages" kept the shape of the carriages they displaced. The void left by surrender first of a supernatural force, and then of Nature (which had replaced Deity during the periods of deistic rationalism) are thus made good. Only gradually did the work of science and the specific conclusions it reached make it clear that science was not a competitor with theology for a single ultimate explanation, so that the justification was no longer resorted to.

The surrender does not mean that search for broad generalizations has been given up. It means that the nature and function of these generalizations have changed. They are now, in effect and function, formulae for effecting transformations from one field to another, the qualitative difference of the fields being maintained. The doctrine of the conservation of energy represents, for example, an exceedingly comprehensive generalization. In terms of the now discarded philosophy of science, it would be said to set up a force which is at once electrical, mechanical, thermal, etc., and yet none of them, but a kind of nondescript Thing-in-itself back of all of them. In actual scientific procedure, it is a formula for converting any one of these forms of energy into any other, provided certain conditions are satisfied.

The same principle holds good of the recently discovered transmutation of chemical elements. It does not wipe out the differences of quality that mark off phenomena from one another but sets forth the conditions under which one kind is changed into another kind. Differences in the practical operations that are based upon science correspond with the change that has come about in theory—as the techniques of modern chemical industry are different from the dreams of the alchemists. No one today would think of undertaking a definite invention, the heavier-than-air flying boat, the internal combustion engine, and so on, by setting out from an alleged universal law of the working of some single ultimate force. The inventor who translates an idea into a working technological device starts from examination of special materials and tries special methods for combining them.

The practical techniques derived from the Marxist single all-embracing law of a single causative force follow the pattern discarded in scientific inquiry and in scientific engineering. What is necessary according to it is to promote class war in as great a variety of ways and on as many occasions as possible. For the essence of the theory, according to the dialectical method, is not recognition of class conflicts as *facts*—in which respect it provided a needed correction of the early nineteenth century notion of universal harmony and universal interdependence. Its distinguishing trait is that social progress is made by intensifying the conflict between the capitalistic employing classes and the proletarian employed class, so that the supreme principle of morals is to strengthen the power of the latter class.

The physical analogy is about like this: suppose that there had once been a theory that "nature abhors friction." It is then discovered that no mechanical work is done without resistance, and that there is no resistance without friction. It is then concluded that by abolishing lubrication and magnifying friction, a state of universal friction will by its own inner dialectic result in an adjustment of energies to one another which will provide the best possible conditions for doing useful work. Society *is* marked by conflict and friction of interests; interests may by some stretching and more consolidation be used to define classes. It may also be admitted that the conflict between them has under certain conditions served as a stimulus to social progress; it might even be admitted that a society in which there was no opposition of interests would be sunk in a condition of hopeless lethargy. But the idea of obtaining universal harmony by the greatest possible intensification of conflicts would remain analogous to the physical illustration given. Persons who are not Marxists often identify the proposition that serious strife of economic interests exists with the genuine Marxist thesis that it is the sole agency by which social change is effected in the desirable direction of a classless society.

The criticism made is not directed then to any generalization made by Marx on the basis of observation of actual conditions. On the contrary, the implication of the criticism is the necessity for *continued* observation of actual conditions, with testing and revision of all earlier generalization on the basis of what is now observed. The inherent theoretical weakness of Marxism is that it supposed a generalization that was made at a particular date and place (and made even then only by bringing observed facts under a premise drawn from a metaphysical source) can obviate the need for continued resort to observation, and to continual revision of generalizations in their office of working hypotheses. In the name of science, a thoroughly anti-scientific procedure was formulated, in accord with which a generalization is made having the nature of ultimate "truth," and hence holding good at all times and places.

Laissez-faire individualism indulged in the same kind of sweeping generalization but in the opposite direction. Doubtless, in accordance with the law of the union of opposites, this background played its part in creating a cultural atmosphere favorable to Marxism. But two opposite errors do not constitute one truth, especially when both errors have the same root. With some disregard for historic facts, the Marxist doctrine might even be regarded as a generalized version of that aspect of classic economic theory which held that completely free competition in the open market would automatically produce universal harmony of persons and nations, Marx converting competition of individuals into war of classes.

Marxism has, then, been selected as an illustration of the monistic block-universe theory of social causation. A few years ago the laissez-faire view, developed out of ideas of Adam Smith when they were wedded to ideas of utilitarian morals and psychology, would have been appropriately taken. The Russian Revolution is chiefly accountable for having brought Marxism to the foreground. Being conducted in the name of Marx, it claimed to be a large scale demonstration of the validity of the Marxist theory. The Union of Soviet Socialist Republics has fastened attention upon the theory as no idea ever succeeds on its own account in obtaining notice. It caused Marxism to be a terrifying menace in some quarters while giving it enormous prestige in other quarters. It led to a disruption of old socialist parties, as the Russian Revolution was held up in other countries as proof of the Marxist theory of class war and the dictatorship of the proletariat. The issue raised by events in Russia gave actuality to Marxist doctrine in every country of the globe.

An event of this sort cannot occur without arousing intense feeling, and corresponding conflicts of interpretation. In the present case, the division extends not only to the theory but to the facts of the situation. One can find data, real or alleged, to support almost any view as to the actual situation in the U.S.S.R., according to the source one takes to be authoritative. Facts, including statistics, are cited to show that extraordinary progress has been made in industrialization of the country and mechanization of agricultural pursuits, with an immense gain in productivity, and, what is more important, in creation of a genuine workers' republic, attended with striking rise in the material and cultural standards of living of the great mass of the population. But one may also find evidence to support the view that the dictatorship of the proletariat became first that of a party over the proletariat and then the dictatorship of a small band of bureaucrats over the party, until the latter, to maintain power, has adopted, with greatly improved technical skill in execution, all the repressive measures of the overthrown Czarist despotism. One can find evidence that, under a regime of governmental, instead of social, control, economic classes marked by great inequality of income are growing up. Such questions of fact are not settled by argument. Hence though there is no doubt in my own mind as to the conclusion available evidence points to, I shall not here attempt to take a stand on the particular issues of fact which are involved.

Certain facts that are not denied suffice as far as the present topic and problem are concerned. A monistic theory is accompanied in its practical execution by one-party control of press, schools, radio, the theater and every means of communication, even to effective restrictions imposed on private gatherings and private conversations. One of the reasons for the great difference in opinion about the state of facts—the point just mentioned—is the fact that effective dictatorship (and an ineffective dictatorship is not a dictatorship at all) exercises complete command over the press, over travel, over letters and personal communications. In consequence, only a few have access to the sources of information about political methods, and that few is just the group with the greatest interest in preventing free inquiry and report.

This suppression of freedom of belief and of speech, press and assembly is not among the facts in dispute for it is of the essence of the dictatorship, which in turn is of the essence of the doctrine the Revolution claims to have put in force. Nor is ruthless persecution and punishment of all dissenters one of the disputed facts. A succession of trials has eliminated from life (as well as from political action) every one of the men and women who brought on the Revolution, save a few relatively minor characters. The *justification* of the action is one of the things in controversy, but not the fact of the exile, imprisonment or execution of every important earlier leader. As a criterion for judging the theory back of revolutionary method of class war, it would not seem to make a great deal of difference whether we decide these men were traitors to their own cause of the liberation of humanity, or are victims of the desire of a clique to keep in their hands a monopoly of all power—great as will be the difference in our judgment about the character of the persons involved.

Events not in dispute confirm the conclusion drawn from other historical instances that absolute principles are intolerant of dissent, for dissent from "The Truth" is more than an intellectual error. It is proof of an evil and dangerous will. When the dominant dogma is definitely theological, the evil will is described in one set of terms; when it is political, the phraseology is different, "counter-revolution" taking the place of "heresy."

The psychological and moral dispositions stimulated and the

kind of activities in which they are expressed are extraordinarily similar. No general theory, moreover, is self-translating in application to particular events. Some body of persons must exist to state just what its significance is in its bearing upon this and that situation, and a body that merely interprets is impotent unless it has power to enforce decisions. The extreme danger of giving any body of persons power for whose exercise they are not accountable is a commonplace in a democracy. Arbitrary irresponsibility varies in direct ratio to the claim for absoluteness on the part of the principle in behalf of which power is exercised. To sustain the principle against heresy, or counter-revolutionary action, it finally becomes necessary to clothe the human officials that are supposed to represent the principle with the finality of the professed end. Divinity once hedged about kings. An earlier repudiation in Russia of glorification of individual persons, because of the immensely superior importance of collective action, gives way to Byzantine adulation of the Leader.

That the state, as governmental coercive power, is not withering away is another indisputable fact. Instead there has been an increase of the intensity and range of state action; the independent activity of factions within the party, of trade unions and of the original soviets is now judged to be, if not counter-revolutionary, at least hostile to the maintenance of the dictatorship of the proletariat. It is a part of original Marxist doctrine that no class having power surrenders it without being compelled to do so by superior force. The application of this particular phase of the doctrine to those who now wield power is one of the "contradictions" attending the dialectical theory. It might be worth while to ask whether the constant splintering of professed Marxists into factions that fight one another as bitterly as they fight their professed foe does not bear a similar relation to the doctrine of class war.

For while it was part of the original doctrine that personal hatred is outside the scope of the impersonal sweep of economic forces, it is doubtful if there is any case in history of *odium theologicum* that surpasses in intensity the venom displayed by convinced disciples of the orthodox Marxist creed toward dissenters, the venom being even greater against those who agree in some respects than towards professed representatives of capitalism. For the former are heretics, while the latter are simply believers in a faith that is natural to them. Like pagans, as distinct from heretics, they do not know any better. Verbal abuse in countries like the United States is the substitute for the physical power exerted where dictatorship exists, the mildest epithet being that of Fascist or friend of Fascism.

The large measure of sympathy shown by liberals in our own country toward Russian totalitarianism—to the extent of asserting the country is essentially a democracy with which common cause should be made against Fascist states—is not surprising. There are undoubted advances made in many directions in the U.S.S.R., since the overthrow of Czardom. They are visible and well-publicized, while the conduct of political affairs is a sealed book. More influential still is the fact that those persons who see the obstructive power of the existing economic system in our country are moved by the fact that one country has done something about overthrowing that system. Also we are not in the habit of taking social and political philosophies very seriously. We take them empirically and "pragmatically," as useful rallying-cries. We do not realize that continental Europeans, especially those educated under the influence of German ideas, have a still greater contempt for action which is "empirically" directed than we have for abstract theory. Again, when events occur that are obviously unfortunate, it is easy to explain them as a result of survival of tendencies bred in the earlier despotism or as expressions of a mentality which is still quasi-Asiatic—although in fact these are the attitudes which have made it possible for a monolithic theory of the Marxist type to flourish.

While nothing said discounts the effect of economic factors upon other components of culture (and certainly not upon political ones at the present time), nevertheless democratic methods are proved, even if they lack adequate substance, to be indispensable to effecting economic change in the interest of freedom. In common with many others, I have from time to time pointed out the harmful consequences the present regime of industry and finance has upon the reality of democratic ends and methods. I have nothing to retract. But conditions in totalitarian countries have brought home the fact, not sufficiently realized by critics, myself included, that the forms which still exist encourage freedom of discussion, criticism and voluntary associations, and thereby set a gulf between a country having suffrage and popular representation and a country having dictatorships, whether of the right or left—the differences between the two latter growing continually less as they borrow each other's techniques.

The Marxist theory holds that government in so-called democratic states is only the organ of a capitalist class, using legislatures, courts, army and police to do its will and maintain its class supremacy. But the effect of constant criticism of governmental action; of more than one political party in formulating rival policies; of frequent elections; of the discussion and public education that attend majority rule, and above all the fact that political action is but one factor in the interplay of a number of cultural factors, have a value that critics of partial democracy have not realized. And this point is strengthened when we accept the criticism that much of our political democracy is more formal than substantial, provided it is placed in contrast with totalitarian political control. Subordination of the political to the economic has a meaning for those trained to take for granted the operation of an indefinite plurality of social tendencies, many of which are neither political nor economic, that it cannot possibly have in countries that are without the democratic tradition. It is difficult for even English people to understand why and how it is that politics are not the absorbing interest in this country they are in England. If the result with us is often looseness of cohesion and indefiniteness in direction of action, there is generated a certain balance of judgment and some sort of equilibrium in social affairs. We take for granted the action of a number of diverse factors in producing any social result. There are temporary waves of insistence upon this and that particular measure and aim. But there is at least enough democracy so that in time any one tendency gets averaged up in interplay with other tendencies. An average presents qualities that are open to easy criticism. But as compared with the fanaticism generated by monistic ideas when they are put into operation, the averaging of tendencies, a movement toward a mean, is an achievement of splendor. However, the habit of imagination that is bred makes it easier than it otherwise would be to idealize conditions in a country which, like Russia, aims at a monolithic structure. The "common man" may be common but for that reason he strikes a certain balance, and the balance struck is a greater safeguard of democracy than any particular law can be, even if written into the Constitution.

The experimental method of science [handwritten annotation in top margin]

The moral is not unintelligent glorification of empirical, pluralistic, and pragmatic method. On the contrary, the lesson to be learned is the importance of ideas and of a plurality of ideas employed in experimental activity as working hypotheses. Thoughtless empiricism provides opportunity for secret manipulation behind the visible scene. When we assume that we are following common sense policies, in the most honorable sense of common sense, we may in fact, unless we direct observation of conditions by means of general ideas, be in process of being led around by the nose by agencies purporting to be democratic, but whose activities are subversive of freedom: a generalized warning which, when translated into concrete words, should make us wary toward those who talk glibly about the "American way of life," after they have identified Americanism with a partisan policy in behalf of concealed economic aims.

The experimental method of science is the exemplification of empirical method when experience has reached maturity. It is opposed equally to "vulgar" empiricism which recognizes only rule-of-thumb action, depending upon a succession of trial-and-error acts that are unregulated by connection with an idea which is both expressed and tested, and to that absolutism which insists there is but one Truth and that truth one already revealed and possessed by some group or party. Mr. John Strachey, an Englishman, not a Russian, may be quoted upon the extent to which present "Communist" thought is authoritarian and monistic—that is, ruled by an ideal of uniformity. For he says that communistic parties even outside of Russia, e.g., in this country, in "refusal to tolerate the co-existence of incompatible opinions . . . are simply asserting the claim that socialism is scientific." It would be difficult, probably impossible, to find a more direct and elegantly finished denial of all the qualities that make ideas and theories either scientific or democratic than is contained in this statement. It helps explain why literary persons have been chiefly the ones in this country who have fallen for Marxist theory, since they are the ones who, having the least amount of scientific attitude, swallow most readily the notion that "science" is a new kind of infallibility.

To repeat a statement already made in another connection, no generalization which, like Marxism, claims to state the final truth about changes (whether physical or social), can set forth the significance of the general idea that is accepted in connection with actual events as they happen. For the purpose of day by day *action,* the sole value of a theory is the significance given to concrete events, when they are viewed in the light of the theory, in the concrete relations they sustain to one another. It is no accident that the final effect of uniformity of ideas is to set up some selected body of persons above the theoretical generalization. Those who determine what the theory signifies in terms of the one important thing—namely, *what should be done*—are supreme over the theory even when they claim to act in subjection to it. The demand for uniformity of opinion, "the refusal to tolerate the existence of incompatible opinions," demands first that there be a party and then a select council of persons within the party, to decide just what after all is The Truth with respect to events as they arise—together with a truly theological technique of exegesis to explain the perfect consistency existing among a succession of inconsistent policies. Thus there has been the change from the earlier denunciation of democracy as identical with middle class capitalism and the labeling of all other socialists as Social-Fascists, to the present policy of a Popular Front, and to the presentation of Bolshevism as twentieth century democracy. And, again, change from denunciation of Nazi Germany to the beginnings of a virtual alliance with it, but now in the wholly praiseworthy interest of world peace, following upon the former orthodox doctrine that only communism can institute peace after a succession of wars international and civil. Scientific method in operating with working hypotheses instead of with fixed and final Truth is not forced to have an Inner Council to declare just what is the Truth nor to develop a system of exegesis which rivals the ancient theological way of explaining away apparent inconsistencies. It welcomes a clash of "incompatible opinions" as long as they can produce observed facts in their support.

Since Marxism has been taken as the example of a uniformitarian theory, basing itself upon "objective" factors of the environment in separation from their interaction with the factors of human nature, something will be said in closing about the ignoring of human qualities. For it contradicts the statement sometimes made that the essence of Marxism, at least as a practical doctrine, is appeal to the motive of self-interest. This statement is made as an accusation by non-Marxists, while it sometimes appears in what profess to be Marxist documents. But actually it comes close to reversing actual Marxist doctrine—the doctrine that the state of the forces of production is the sole causal force. For according to this view, all the factors of human nature are shaped from without by "materialistic," that is economic, forces. To give independent validity to any component of human nature would be, from the Marxist standpoint, a relapse into the "idealistic" type of theory that Marxism came to destroy.

A much juster criticism would be that Marxism systematically neglects everything on the side of human nature with respect to its being a factor having efficacy, save as it is previously determined by the state of the forces of production. In claiming to replace "Utopian" socialisms, Marxism throws out psychological as well as moral considerations. Whether the theory is in fact able to live up to this claim—without which its "materialism" is meaningless—is another matter. For it would seem as if certain organic needs and appetites at least were required to set the "forces of production" moving. But if this bio-psychological factor is admitted, then it must *interact* with "external" factors, and there is no particular point at which its operation can be said to cease.

The point involved has a practical as well as theoretical force. Take for example the matter of classes and of class-*consciousness*, the latter being an imperatively required condition in the Marxist theory. According to orthodox Marxism, the class consciousness of the proletariat is generated by the fact that the state of economic forces represented by large-scale factory production throws wage-workers closely together with little or no direct intercourse with employers—such as existed, for example, in shops where hand tools were used. Physical conditions thus demarcate economic classes, and throw into relief the conflict of interests between employers and employees, together with the community of interests, if only in misery, that bind together the latter. Now as an observation there is an undeniable element of truth in this position—especially in contrast with the favorite editorial exhortation that there can be no conflict between "Capital" and "Labor" since each depends on the other. But the facts involved in the observation are not compatible with the ultimate theory. The formation of a class, especially of class consciousness, depends upon the operation of psychological factors which are not mentioned—and which the theory rules out.

The fact is that Marx and every Marxist after him unconsciously assumes the existence and operation of factors in the constitution of human nature which must cooperate with "external" economic or "material" conditions in producing what actually happens. Explicit recognition of these factors would give the theory a different practical slant. It would have put the things emphasized by Marx in a different perspective. The fact seems to be that Marx himself unconsciously took over the current psychology of his time, standing also on *its* head the optimistic psychology of laissez-faire liberalism. Overt recognition of the psychological factors entails introduction of values and judgments of valuation into a theory of social movement—as is shown later.

Any monolithic theory of social action and social causation tends to have a ready-made answer for problems that present themselves. The wholesale character of this answer prevents critical examination and discrimination of the particular facts involved in the actual problem. In consequence, it dictates a kind of all-or-none practical activity, which in the end introduces new difficulties. I suggest as illustrations two sets of events that have played a great part in the history of the U.S.S.R. According to the theory, the members of the agricultural class, as far as they own land, belong to the bourgeoisie, although of the "petty" subdivision. Only factory workers, congregated in cities, belong to the proletariat. By theory then class war exists between city workers and most of the rural population. There is a genuine psychological and political problem involved in getting these two groups of human beings together for common social action. But the wholesale or monistic character of the theoretical premise prevents exploration of the problem *as* a problem. It is settled in advance that the class conflict is of such a nature that success of the revolutionary movement is bound up with domination of the urban wage worker over the rural population. Anybody who has followed Russian history knows that an already difficult problem has been tremendously exacerbated by acceptance of this absolute principle—in spite of considerable flexibility on Lenin's part in applying it.

The other example is the question of the possibility of building socialism in one country at a time when the state of forces of production is international. Here again there is a difficult problem with respect to the policies to be adopted in adjusting domestic and foreign relations. The all-or-none theory led in Russia to a complete political break-up in the formation of two completely hostile factions within the original Communist Party. Negotiations, compromise, working out of a policy on the basis of study of actual conditions was ruled out in advance. Even when the original orthodox Marxism was abandoned in favor of an effort to build socialism in one country—a policy for which on practical grounds a great deal could be said—it had to be proved that this policy was the one and the only one authorized by the all-or-none theory which cannot "tolerate incompatible opinions" because of the "scientific" character of the doctrine. The most effective way of proving the point was to behead all those who took a contrary view as traitors and counter-revolutionaries.

It is ironical that the theory which has made the most display and the greatest pretense of having a scientific foundation should be the one which has violated most systematically every principle of scientific method. What we may learn from the contradiction is the potential alliance between scientific and democratic method and the need of consummating this potentiality in the techniques of legislation and administration. It is of the nature of science not so much to tolerate as to welcome diversity of opinion, while it insists that inquiry brings the evidence of observed facts to bear to effect a consensus of conclusions—and even then to hold the conclusion subject to what is ascertained and made public in further new inquiries. I would not claim that any existing democracy has ever made complete or adequate use of scientific method in deciding upon its policies. But freedom of inquiry, toleration of diverse views, freedom of communication, the distribution of what is found out to every individual as the ultimate intellectual consumer, are involved in the democratic as in the scientific method. When democracy openly recognizes the existence of *problems* and the need for probing them *as* problems as its glory, it will relegate political groups that pride themselves upon refusing to admit incompatible opinions to the obscurity which already is the fate of similar groups in science.

5. Democracy and Human Nature

[handwritten marginalia: Interest of h. nature correspond to assertion of political rights of people]

It is not accidental that the rise of interest in human nature coincided in time with the assertion in political matters of the rights of the people as a whole, over against the rights of a class supposedly ordained by God or Nature to exercise rule. The full scope and depth of the connection between assertion of democracy in government and new consciousness of human nature cannot be presented without going into an opposite historic background, in which social arrangements and political forms were taken to be an expression of Nature—but most decidedly not of *human* nature. There would be involved an account, upon the side of theory, of the long history of the idea of *Laws of Nature* from the time of Aristotle and the Stoics to the formulators of modern jurisprudence in the sixteenth and seventeenth centuries.

The story of this development and of the shift, in the eighteenth century, from Natural Law to Natural Rights is one of the most important chapters in the intellectual and moral history of mankind. But to delve into it would here take us too far away from the immediate theme. I must content myself then with emphatic reassertion of the statement that regard for *human* nature as the source of legitimate political arrangements is comparatively late in European history; that when it arose it marked an almost revolutionary departure from previous theories about the basis of political rule and citizenship and subjection—so much so that the fundamental difference between even ancient republican and modern democratic governments has its source in the substitution of human nature for cosmic nature as the foundation of politics. Finally changes and the need for further change in democratic theory are connected with an inadequate theory of the constitution of human nature and its component elements in their relation to social phenomena.

The subject matter which follows is that of a drama in thre‍
acts, of which the last is the unfinished one now being enacted in
which we, now living, are the participants. The first act, as far as
it is possible to tell its condensed story, is that of a one-sided simplification of human nature which was used to promote and justify the new political movement. The second act is that of the
reaction against the theory and the practices connected with it,
on the ground that it was the forerunner of moral and social anarchy, the cause of dissolution of the ties of cohesion that bind
human beings together in organic union. The third act, now
playing, is that of recovery of the moral significance of the connection of human nature and democracy, now stated in concrete
terms of existing conditions and freed from the one-sided exag-
gerations of the earlier statement. I give this summary first because in what follows I have been compelled to go in some detail
into matters that if pursued further are technically theoretical.

I begin by saying that the type of theory which isolated the
"external" factor of interactions that produce social phenomena
is paralleled by one which isolated the "internal" or human factor. Indeed, if I had followed the historic order the latter type of
theory would have been discussed first. And this type of theory is
still more widely and influentially held than we might suppose.
For its vogue is not now adequately represented by those professional psychologists and sociologists who claim that all social
phenomena are to be understood in terms of the mental operations of individuals, since society consists in the last analysis only
of individual persons. The practically effective statement of the
point of view is found in economic theory, where it furnished the
backbone of laissez-faire economics; and in the British political
liberalism which developed in combination with this economic
doctrine. A particular view of human motives in relation to social events, as explanations of them and as the basis of all sound
social policy, has not come to us labeled psychology. But as a theory about human nature it is essentially psychological. We still
find a view put forth as to an intrinsic and necessary connection
between democracy and capitalism which has a psychological
foundation and temper. For it is only because of belief in a certain theory of human nature that the two are said to be Siamese
twins, so that attack upon one is a threat directed at the life of
the other.

The classic expression of the point of view which would explain social phenomena by means of psychological phenomena is that of John Stuart Mill in his *Logic*—a statement that probably appeared almost axiomatic when it was put forth. "All phenomena of society are phenomena of human nature . . . and if therefore the phenomena of human thought, feeling and action are subject to fixed laws, the phenomena of society cannot but conform to law." And again, "The laws of the phenomena of society are and can be nothing but the laws of the actions and passions of human beings united in the social state." And then, as if to state conclusively that being "united in the social state" makes no difference as to the laws of individuals and hence none in those of society, he adds, "Human beings in society have no properties but those which are derived from and may be resolved into the laws of the nature of individual man."

This reference to "individual man" discloses the nature of the particular simplification which controlled the views and the policies of this particular school. The men who expressed and entertained the type of philosophy whose method was summed up by Mill were in their time revolutionaries. They wished to liberate a certain group of individuals, those concerned in new forms of industry, commerce and finance, from shackles inherited from feudalism which were endeared by custom and interest to a powerful landed aristocracy. If they do not appear now to be revolutionary (operating to bring about social change by change in men's opinions not by force), it is because their views are now the philosophy of conservatives in every highly industrialized country.

They essayed an intellectual formulation of principles which would justify the success of the tendencies which present day revolutionaries call the bourgeois capitalism they are trying to overthrow. The psychology in question is not that of present textbooks. But it expressed the individualistic ideas that animated the economic and political theories of the radicals of the time. Its "individualism" supplied the background of a great deal of even the technical psychology of the present day—pretty much all of it, save that which has started on a new tack because of biological and anthropological considerations. At the time of its origin, it was not a bookish doctrine even when written down in books. The books were elaborations of ideas that were propounded in electoral campaigns and offered as laws to be adopted by parliament.

Before engaging in any detailed statements, I want to recall a statement made earlier; namely, that the popular view of the constitution of human nature at any given time is a reflex of social movements which have either become institutionalized or else are showing themselves against opposing social odds and hence need intellectual and moral formulation to increase their power. I may seem to be going far afield if I refer to Plato's statement of the way by which to determine the constituents of human nature. The proper method, he said, was to look at the version of human nature written in large and legible letters in the organization of classes in society, before trying to make it out in the dim petty edition found in individuals. And so on the basis of the social organization with which he was acquainted he found that since in society there was a laboring class toiling to find the means of satisfying the appetites, a citizen soldiery class loyal even to death to the laws of the state, and a legislative class, so the human soul must be composed of appetite at the base—in both significations of "base"—of generous spirited impulses which looked beyond personal enjoyment, while appetite was engaged only in taking in and absorbing for its own satisfaction, and finally reason, the legislative power.

Having found these three things in the composition of human nature, he had no difficulty in going back to social organization and proving that there was one class which had to be kept in order by rules and laws imposed from above, since otherwise its action was without limits, and would in the name of liberty destroy harmony and order; another class, whose inclinations were all towards obedience and loyalty to law, towards right beliefs, although itself incapable of discovering the ends from which laws are derived; and at the apex, in any well-ordered organization, the rule of those whose predominant natural qualities were reason, after that faculty had been suitably formed by education.

It would be hard to find a better illustration of the fact that any movement purporting to discover the psychological causes and sources of social phenomena is in fact a reverse movement, in which current social tendencies are read back into the structure of human nature; and are then used to explain the very things from which they are deduced. It was then "natural" for the men who reflected the new movement of industry and commerce to erect the appetites, treated by Plato as a kind of necessary evil, into the cornerstone of social well-being and progress. Something of the same kind exists at present when love of power is put forward to play the role taken a century ago by self-interest as the dominant "motive"—and if I put the word motive in quotation marks, it is for the reason just given. What are called motives turn out upon critical examination to be complex attitudes patterned under cultural conditions, rather than simple elements in human nature.

Even when we refer to tendencies and impulses that actually are genuine elements in human nature we find, unless we swallow whole some current opinion, that of themselves they explain nothing about social phenomena. For they produce consequences only as they are shaped into acquired dispositions by interaction with environing cultural conditions. Hobbes, who was the first of the moderns to identify the "state of nature" and its laws— the classic background of all political theories—with the raw uneducated state of human nature, may be called as witness. According to Hobbes, "In the nature of man we find three principal causes of quarrel. First competition, secondly diffidence, thirdly glory. The first maketh men invade for gain; the second for safety; and the third for reputation. The first use violence to make themselves the masters of other persons; the second to defend them; the third for trifles as a word, a smile, a different opinion or any other sign of undervalue, either direct in their persons or by reflection in their kindred, their friends, their nation."

That the qualities mentioned by Hobbes actually exist in human nature and that they may generate "quarrel," that is, conflict and war between states and civil war within a nation—the chronic state of affairs when Hobbes lived—is not denied. Insofar, Hobbes' account of the natural psychology which prevents the state of security which is a pre-requisite for civilized communities shows more insight than many attempts made today to list the traits of raw human nature that are supposed to cause social phenomena. Hobbes thought that the entire natural state of men in their relations to one another was a war of all against all, man being naturally to man "as a wolf." The intent of Hobbes was thus a glorification of deliberately instituted relations, authoritative laws and regulations which should rule not just overt actions, but the impulses and ideas which cause men to hold up certain things as ends or goods. Hobbes himself thought of this authority as a political sovereign. But it would be in the spirit of his treatment to regard it as glorification of culture over against raw human nature, and more than one writer has pointed out the likeness between his Leviathan and the Nazi totalitarian state.

There are more than one instructive parallelisms that may be drawn between the period in which Hobbes lived and the present time, especially as to insecurity and conflict between nations and classes. The point here pertinent, however, is that the qualities Hobbes selected as the causes of disorders making the life of mankind "brutish and nasty," are the very "motives" that have been selected by others as the cause of *beneficent* social effects; namely, harmony, prosperity, and indefinite progress. The position taken by Hobbes about competition as love of gain was completely reversed in the British social philosophy of the nineteenth century. Instead of being a source of war, it was taken to be the means by which individuals found the occupation for which they were best fitted; by which needed goods reached the consumer at least cost, and by which a state of ultimate harmonious interdependence would be produced—provided only competition were allowed to operate without "artificial" restriction. Even today one reads articles and hears speeches in which the cause of our present economic troubles is laid to political interference with the beneficent workings of private competitive effort for gain.

The object of alluding to these two very different conceptions of this component in human nature is not to decide or discuss which is right. The point is that both are guilty of the same fallacy. In itself, the impulse (or whatever name be given it) is neither socially maleficent nor beneficent. Its significance depends upon consequences actually produced; and these depend upon the conditions under which it operates and with which it interacts. The conditions are set by tradition, by custom, by law, by the kind of public approvals and disapprovals; by all conditions constituting the environment. These conditions are so pluralized even in one and the same country at the same period that love of gain (regarded as a trait of human nature) may be both socially useful and socially harmful. And, in spite of the tendency to set up cooperative impulses as thoroughly beneficial, the same thing is true of them—regarded simply as components of human nature. Neither competition nor cooperation can be judged as traits of human nature. They are names for certain relations among the actions of individuals as the relations actually obtain in a community.

This would be true even if there were tendencies in human nature so definitely marked off from one another as to merit the names given them and even if human nature were as fixed as it is sometimes said to be. For even in that case, human nature operates in a multitude of different environing conditions, and it is interaction with the latter that determines the consequences and the social significance and value, positive or negative, of the tendencies. The alleged fixity of the structure of human nature does not explain in the least the differences that mark off one tribe, family, people, from another—which is to say that in and of itself it explains no state of society whatever. It issues no advice as to what policies it is advantageous to follow. It does not even justify conservatism as against radicalism.

But the alleged unchangeableness of human nature cannot be admitted. For while certain needs in human nature are constant, the consequences they produce (because of the existing state of culture—of science, morals, religion, art, industry, legal rules) react back into the original components of human nature to shape them into new forms. The total pattern is thereby modified. The futility of exclusive appeal to psychological factors both to explain what takes place and to form policies as to what *should* take place, would be evident to everybody—had it not proved to be a convenient device for "rationalizing" policies that are urged on other grounds by some group or faction. While the case of "competition" urging men both to war and to beneficent social progress is most obviously instructive in this respect, examination of the other elements of Hobbes supports the same conclusion.

There have been communities, for example, in which regard for the honor of one's self, one's family, one's class, has been the chief conservator of all worth while social values. It has always been the chief virtue of an aristocratic class, civil or military. While its value has often been exaggerated, it is folly to deny that in interaction with certain cultural conditions, it has had valuable consequences. "Diffidence" or fear as a motive is an even more ambiguous and meaningless term as far as its consequences are concerned. It takes any form, from craven cowardice to prudence, caution, and the circumspection without which no intelligent foresight is possible. It may become reverence—which has been exaggerated in the abstract at times but which may be attached to the kind of objects which render it supremely desirable. "Love of power," to which it is now fashionable to appeal, has a meaning only when it applies to everything in general and hence explains nothing in particular.

Discussion up to this point has been intended to elicit two principles. One of them is that the views about human nature that are popular at a given time are usually derived from contemporary social currents; currents so conspicuous as to stand out or else less marked and less effective social movements which a special group believes *should* become dominant:—as for example, in the case of the legislative reason with Plato, and of competitive love of gain with classical economists. The other principle is that reference to components of original human nature, even if they actually exist, explains no social occurrence whatever and gives no advice or direction as to what policies it is better to adopt. This does not mean that reference to them must necessarily be of a "rationalizing" concealed apologetic type. It means that whenever it occurs with practical significance it has *moral* not psychological import. For, whether brought forward from the side of conserving what already exists or from that of producing change, it is an expression of valuation, and of purpose determined by estimate of values. When a trait of human nature is put forward on this basis, it is in its proper context and is subject to intelligent examination.

The prevailing habit, however, is to assume that a social issue does not concern values to be preferred and striven for, but rather something predetermined by the constitution of human nature. This assumption is the source of serious social ills. Intellectually it is a reversion to the type of explanation that governed physical science until say, the seventeenth century: a method now seen to have been the chief source of the long-continued retardation of natural science. For this type of theory consists of appeal to general forces to "explain" what happens.

Natural science began to progress steadily only when general forces were banished and inquiry was directed instead to ascertaining correlations that exist between observed changes. Popular appeal to, say, electricity, light or heat, etc., as a force to account for some particular event still exists, as to electricity to explain storms attended by thunder and lightning. Scientific men themselves often talk in similar words. But such general terms are in their case shorthand expressions. They stand for uniform relations between events that are observed to occur; they do not mark appeal to something behind what happens and which is supposed to produce it. If we take the case of the lightning flash and electricity, Franklin's identification of the former as of the electrical kind brought it into connection with things from which it had been formerly isolated, and knowledge about them was available in dealing with it. But instead of electricity being an explanatory force, knowledge that lightning is an electrical phenomenon opened a number of special problems, some of which are still unsolved.

If the analogy between the relatively sterile condition of natural science when this method prevailed and the present state of the social "sciences" is not convincing, the misdirection of inquiry that results may be cited in evidence. There is an illusion of understanding, when in reality there is only a general word that conceals lack of understanding. Social ideas are kept in the domain of glittering generalities. Opinion as distinct from knowledge breeds controversy. Since what is regarded as a cause is that which is used as an agency or instrumentality of production, there is no controlled method of bringing anything into existence and of preventing the occurrence of that not wanted, save as there is knowledge of the conditions of its occurrence. When men knew that a certain kind of friction produced fire, they had at command at least one means, rubbing of sticks together, for producing fire when they wanted it. And it goes without saying that greater acquaintance with causal conditions has multiplied men's practical ability to have fire when needed, and to use it for an increased number of ends. The principle applies to the relation of social theory and social action.

Finally theories supposed to explain the course of events are used to urge and justify certain practical policies. Marxism is, of course, a striking instance. But it is so far from being the only instance that non-Marxian and anti-Marxian social theories often exemplify the principle. Utilitarianism used the idea that pleasure and pain are the sole determinants of human action to advance a sweeping theory of legislation, judicial and penal procedure; namely, that they be directed to secure the greatest happiness of the greatest number. Explanation of events on the basis of free, unimpeded manifestation of wants was used on the practical side as active propaganda for an open-market economic regime with all political and legal measures adapted to it. Belief in the general character of the alleged "force" rendered it unnecessary to keep track of actual events so as to check the theory. If things happened that obviously went contrary to the creed, the inconsistency was not taken as a reason for examining it, but as the cue for alleging special reasons for the failure, so that the truth of the principle could be kept intact.

Mere general ideas can be argued for and against without the necessity of recourse to observation. The arguments are saved from being a mere matter of words only because there are certain emotional attitudes involved. When general ideas are not capable of being continuously checked and revised by observation of what actually takes place, they are, as a mere truism, in the field of opinion. Clash of opinions is in that case the occasion for controversy, not, as is now the case in natural science, a location of a problem and an occasion for making further observations. If any generalization can be safely laid down about intellectual matters and their consequences, it is that the reign of opinion, and of controversial conflicts, is a function of absence of methods of inquiry which bring new facts to light and by so doing establish the basis for consensus of beliefs.

Social events are sufficiently complex in any case so that the development of effective methods of observation, yielding generalization about correlation of events, is difficult. The prevailing type of theory adds the further handicap of making such observation unnecessary—save as this and that arbitrarily selected event is used in argumentative controversy. The prime necessity is to frame general ideas, first, to promote search for problems— as against the assumption of a ready-made solution in view of which there are no problems; and, secondly, to solve these problems by generalizations that state interactions between analytically observed events.

I return to the particular social philosophy which associates the economic regime actuated by effort to make private profit with the essential conditions of free and democratic institutions. It is not necessary to go back to the theory in its early English formulation at the hands of laissez-faire liberals. For in spite of the discrediting of the philosophy by events, efforts put forth in this country to establish so-called social control of business has led at present to its revival in an extremely naked form. One does not need to endorse the measures for control that are used to be aware of the fallacy of the theory upon which current objections to them are based. The theory is that capitalism, interpreted as the maximum range of free personal opportunity for production and exchange of goods and services is the Siamese twin of democracy. For the former is identical, so it is claimed, with the personal qualities of initiative, independence, vigor, that are the basic conditions of free political institutions. Hence, so it is argued, the check given to the operation of these personal qualities by governmental regulation of business activities is at the same time an attack upon the practical and moral conditions for the existence of political democracy.

I am not concerned here with the merits of the special arguments put forth in behalf of and against the measures employed. The point is that appeal to certain alleged human motivations in a wholesale way, such as "initiative, independence, enterprise" at large, obscures the need for observation of events in the concrete. If and when special events are observed, interpretation of them is predestined instead of growing out of what is observed. By keeping the issues in the realm of opinion, appeal to equally general wholesale views on the other side is promoted. Then we get a kind of head-on conflict between something called "individualism" on one side and "socialism" on the other. Examination of concrete conditions might disclose certain specifiable conditions under which both of the methods vaguely pointed at by these words would operate to advantage.

The current use of the word *enterprise* as an honorific term is especially instructive with regard to the attempt to draw support for policies from a reference to general inherent traits of human nature. For the only legitimate signification of "enterprise" is a neutral one, an *undertaking* the desirability of which is a matter of actual results produced, which accordingly need to be studied in the concrete. But *enterprise* is given the significance of a certain desirable trait of human nature, so that the issue is taken out of the field of observation into that of opinion plus a eulogistic emotion. "Enterprise" like "initiative" and like "industry" can be exerted in behalf of an indefinite number of objects; the words may designate the activities of an Al Capone or a racketeering labor union as well as a socially useful industrial undertaking.

The case is cited in some detail because it provides a striking example, first, of the conversion of an existing mode of social behavior into a psychological property of human nature; and, secondly, conversion of an alleged matter of psychological fact into a principle of value—a moral matter. Social problems that are set by conditions having definite spatial and temporal boundaries— which have to be determined by observation—are made into matters capable of absolute determination without reference to conditions of place and date. Hence they become matters of opinion and controversial argument—and as the latter decides nothing, the final tendency is to appeal to force as the ultimate arbiter.

The theory of the components of human nature used by the intellectual radicals of Great Britain to justify popular government and freedom included more than the self-interest motivation. It was officially held that sympathy with the gains and losses, the pleasures and pains of others, is a native part of the human endowment. The two components, self-interest and sympathy, opposite in quality, were ingeniously linked together in the complete doctrine—occasionally with explicit reference to the supposedly analogous centripetal and centrifugal components of Newtonian celestial mechanics. The self-interest phase supplied the foundation of the theory of public and governmental action; the sympathetic phase took care of the relations of individuals to one another in their private capacities. The doctrine taught that if political institutions were reformed to do away with special privileges and unfair favoritisms, the sympathetic motive would have a vastly enlarged field of effective and successful operation, since bad institutions were the chief cause that led men to find their personal advantage in acts injurious to others.

The theory was even more important in the reaction it called out than in itself. For "organic idealistic" philosophies developed in Germany during the nineteenth century, and now form the theoretical background and justification of totalitarianism. They took their clew and point of departure from the weaknesses of the theories that based politics and morals, in theory and in practice, upon alleged components of human nature. An adequate account of the form and substance of the reaction would take us into matters which cannot be set forth without going into technicalities. But its basis is simple.

The attempt to locate the source of authority of politics and morals in human nature was regarded as the source of anarchy, disorder, and conflict;—an attempt to build social institutions and personal relationships upon the most unstable of shifting quicksands. At the same time, the philosophers who formulated the new view were Protestants and Northerners. Hence their reaction did not move them to urge acceptance of the doctrines of the Roman Church as the bulwark against the dissolving tendencies of ultra-individualistic ideas and policies.

The French Revolution, with its excesses, was uniformly regarded in German thought as the logical outcome of the attempt to locate authority where nothing binding could be found. It was thus taken to be a practical large scale demonstration of the weakness inherent in the position. The most that could be said for the doctrine was what could be said in defense of the French Revolution—it helped to get rid of abuses that had grown up. As a positive and constructive principle, it was a tragic delusion. The statement of the Rights of Man setting forth the official creed of the Revolution was said to be a summary of the false doctrines that had produced all the characteristic evils of the age. The protest, as just said, refused to accept the doctrines of the Church as the basis for its criticisms and for the constructive measures it proposed. It was itself too deeply influenced by the conditions which had produced the individualism against which it revolted. The extent of this influence is why the movement is criticized by representatives of the Hellenic-medieval ideas as itself intensely "subjectivistic." It found the way to "reconcile" freedom and authority, individuality and law, by setting up an Absolute Self, Mind, Spirit, of which human beings are individually partial manifestations, a "truer" and fuller manifestation being found in social institutions, the state and the course of history. Since history is the final court of judgment and since it represents the movement of absolute Spirit, appeal to force to settle issues between nations is not "really" an appeal to force, but rather to the ultimate logic of absolute reason. The individualistic movement was a necessary transitional movement to bring men to recognition of the primacy and ultimacy of Spirit and Personality in the constitution of nature, man, and society. German organic idealism was to save all that is true in the movement, while eliminating its errors and dangers by lifting it up to the plane of absolute Self and Spirit. There is much that is technical in the movement; much of its detail can be explained only on the ground of special intellectual events. But its heart and core is found in its attempt to find a "higher" justification for individuality and freedom where the latter are merged with law and authority, which *must* be rational since they are manifestations of Absolute Reason. Contemporary totalitarianism has no difficulty in discovering that the Germanic racial spirit embodied in the German state is an adequate substitute, for all practical purposes, for the Hegelian Absolute Spirit.

Rousseau is usually, and in many respects properly, regarded as the prophet and intellectual progenitor of the French Revolution. But by one of those ironies with which history abounds he was also a step-father of the theory that came to full expression in Germany. He served in this capacity partly indirectly by his attack on culture which, as previously said, was the challenge that resulted in glorification of culture over against human nature. But he also acted positively and directly. For in his political writings he advanced the idea that a Common Will is the source of legitimate political institutions; that freedom and law are one and the same thing in the operations of the Common Will, for it must act for the Common Good and hence for the "real" or true Good of every individual.

If the latter set up their purely personal desires against the General Will, it was accordingly legitimate (indeed necessary) to "*force* them to be free." Rousseau intended his theory to state the foundation of self-governing institutions and majority rule. But his premise was employed to prove that the Common—or Universal—Will and Reason was embodied in the national state. Its most adequate incarnation was in those states in which the authority of law, order, and discipline had not been weakened by democratic heresies:—a view which was used in Germany after the Napoleonic conquest to create an aggressive national spirit in that country, one which provided the basis for systematic depreciation of French "materialistic" civilization as over against

German *Kultur*—a depreciation later extended to condemnation of democratic institutions in any country.

While this brief exposition of the reaction against the individualistic theory of human nature suggests the ground pattern of National Socialism, it also throws some light upon the predicament in which democratic countries find themselves. The fact that the individualistic theory was used a century and more ago to justify political self-government and then aided promotion of its cause does not constitute the theory a present trustworthy guide of democratic action. It is profitable to read today the bitterly vivid denunciations of Carlyle on the theory as it was originally put forth. He denounced with equal fierceness the attempt to erect political authority upon the basis of self-interest and private morals upon the exercise of sympathy. The latter was sentimentalism run riot and the former was "Anarchy plus the Constable"—the latter being needed to preserve even a semblance of outward order. His plea for discipline and order included even a plea for leadership by select persons.

The present predicament may be stated as follows: Democracy does involve a belief that political institutions and law be such as to take fundamental account of human nature. They must give it freer play than any non-democratic institutions. At the same time, the theory, legalistic and moralistic, about human nature that has been used to expound and justify this reliance upon human nature has proved inadequate. Upon the legal and political side, during the nineteenth century it was progressively overloaded with ideas and practices which have more to do with business carried on for profit than with democracy. On the moralistic side, it has tended to substitute emotional exhortation to act in accord with the Golden Rule for the discipline and the control afforded by incorporation of democratic ideals into *all* the relations of life. Because of lack of an adequate theory of human nature in its relations to democracy, attachment to democratic ends and methods has tended to become a matter of tradition and habit—an excellent thing as far as it goes, but when it becomes routine is easily undermined when change of conditions changes other habits.

Were I to say that democracy needs a new psychology of human nature, one adequate to the heavy demands put upon it by foreign and domestic conditions, I might be taken to utter an academic irrelevancy. But if the remark is understood to mean that democracy has always been allied with humanism, with faith in the potentialities of human nature, and that the present need is vigorous reassertion of this faith, developed in relevant ideas and manifested in practical attitudes, it but continues the American tradition. For belief in the "common man" has no significance save as an expression of belief in the intimate and vital connection of democracy and human nature.

We cannot continue the idea that human nature when left to itself, when freed from external arbitrary restrictions, will tend to the production of democratic institutions that work successfully. We have now to state the issue from the other side. We have to see that democracy means the belief that humanistic culture should prevail; we should be frank and open in our recognition that the proposition is a moral one—like any idea that concerns what *should* be.

Strange as it seems to us, democracy is challenged by totalitarian states of the Fascist variety on moral grounds just as it is challenged by totalitarianisms of the left on economic grounds. We may be able to defend democracy on the latter score, as far as comparative conditions are involved, since up to the present at least the Union of Soviet Socialist Republics has not "caught up" with us, much less "surpassed" us, in material affairs. But defense against the other type of totalitarianism (and perhaps in the end against also the Marxist type) requires a positive and courageous constructive awakening to the significance of faith in human nature for development of every phase of our culture:— science, art, education, morals and religion, as well as politics and economics. No matter how uniform and constant human nature is in the abstract, the conditions within which and upon which it operates have changed so greatly since political democracy was established among us, that democracy cannot now depend upon or be expressed in political institutions alone. We cannot even be certain that they and their legal accompaniments are actually democratic at the present time—for democracy is expressed in the attitudes of human beings and is measured by consequences produced in their lives.

The impact of the humanist view of democracy upon all forms of culture, upon education, science and art, morals and religion, as well as upon industry and politics, saves it from the criticism passed upon moralistic exhortation. For it tells us that we need to examine every one of the phases of human activity to ascertain what effects it has in release, maturing and fruition of the potentialities of human nature. It does not tell us to "re-arm morally" and all social problems will be solved. It says, Find out how all the constituents of our existing culture are operating and then see to it that whenever and wherever needed they be modified in order that their workings may release and fulfill the possibilities of human nature.

It used to be said (and the statement has not gone completely out of fashion) that democracy is a by-product of Christianity, since the latter teaches the infinite worth of the individual human soul. We are now told by some persons that since belief in the soul has been discredited by science, the moral basis for democracy supposed to exist must go into the discard. We are told that if there are reasons for preferring it to other arrangements of the relations of human beings to one another, they must be found in specialized external advantages which outweigh the advantages of other social forms. From a very different quarter, we are told that weakening of the older theological doctrine of the soul is one of the reasons for the eclipse of faith in democracy. These two views at opposite poles give depth and urgency to the question whether there are adequate grounds for faith in the potentialities of human nature and whether they can be accompanied by the intensity and ardor once awakened by religious ideas upon a theological basis. Is human nature intrinsically such a poor thing that the idea is *absurd?* I do not attempt to give any answer, but the word *faith* is intentionally used. For in the long run democracy will stand or fall with the possibility of maintaining the faith and justifying it by works.

Take, for example, the question of intolerance. Systematic hatred and suspicion of any human group, "racial," sectarian, political, denotes deep-seated scepticism about the qualities of human nature. From the standpoint of a faith in the possibilities of human nature possessing religious quality it is blasphemous. It may start by being directed at a particular group, and be supported in name by assigning special reasons why that group is not worthy of confidence, respect, and decent human treatment. But the underlying attitude is one of fundamental distrust of human nature. Hence it spreads from distrust and hatred of a particular group until it may undermine the conviction that any group of persons has any intrinsic right for esteem or recognition—which, then, if it be given, is for some special and external grounds, such as usefulness to our particular interests and ambitions. There is no physical acid which has the corrosive power possessed by intolerance directed against persons because they belong to a group that bears a certain name. Its corrosive potency gains with what it feeds on. An anti-humanist attitude is the essence of every form of intolerance. Movements that begin by stirring up hostility against a group of people end by denying to them all human qualities.

The case of intolerance is used as an illustration of the intrinsic connection between the prospects of democracy and belief in the potentialities of human nature—not for its own sake, important as it is on its own account. How much of our past tolerance was positive and how much of it a toleration equivalent to "standing" something we do not like, "putting up" with something because it involves too much trouble to try to change it? For a good deal of the present reaction against democracy is probably simply the disclosure of a weakness that was there before; one that was covered up or did not appear in its true light. Certainly racial prejudice against Negroes, Catholics, and Jews is no new thing in our life. Its presence among us is an intrinsic weakness and a handle for the accusation that we do not act differently from Nazi Germany.

The greatest practical inconsistency that would be revealed by searching our own habitual attitudes is probably one between the democratic method of forming opinions in political matters and the methods in common use in forming beliefs in other subjects. In theory, the democratic method is persuasion through public discussion carried on not only in legislative halls but in the press, private conversations and public assemblies. The substitution of ballots for bullets, of the right to vote for the lash, is an expression of the will to substitute the method of discussion for the method of coercion. With all its defects and partialities in determination of political decisions, it has worked to keep factional disputes within bounds, to an extent that was incredible a century or more ago. While Carlyle could bring his gift of satire into play in ridiculing the notion that men by talking to and at each other in an assembly hall can settle what is true in social affairs any more than they can settle what is true in the multiplication table, he failed to see that if men had been using clubs to maim and kill one another to decide the product of 7 times 7, there would have been sound reasons for appealing to discussion and persuasion even in the latter case. The fundamental reply is that social "truths" are so unlike mathematical truths that unanimity of uniform belief is possible in respect to the former only when a dictator has the power to tell others what they must believe—or profess they believe. The adjustment of interests demands that diverse interests have a chance to articulate themselves.

The real trouble is that there is an intrinsic split in our habitual attitudes when we profess to depend upon discussion and persuasion in politics and then systematically depend upon other methods in reaching conclusions in matters of morals and religion, or in anything where we depend upon a person or group possessed of "authority." We do not have to go to theological matters to find examples. In homes and in schools, the places where the essentials of character are supposed to be formed, the usual procedure is settlement of issues, intellectual and moral, by appeal to the "authority" of parent, teacher, or textbook. Dispositions formed under such conditions are so inconsistent with the democratic method that in a crisis they may be aroused to act in positively anti-democratic ways for anti-democratic ends; just as resort to coercive force and suppression of civil liberties are readily palliated in nominally democratic communities when the cry is raised that "law and order" are threatened.

It is no easy matter to find adequate authority for action in the demand, characteristic of democracy, that conditions be such as will enable the potentialities of human nature to reach fruition. Because it is not easy the democratic road is the hard one to take. It is the road which places the greatest burden of responsibility upon the greatest number of human beings. Backsets and deviations occur and will continue to occur. But that which is its weakness at particular times is its strength in the long course of human history. Just because the cause of democratic freedom is the cause of the fullest possible realization of human potentialities, the latter when they are suppressed and oppressed will in time rebel and demand an opportunity for manifestation. With the founders of American democracy, the claims of democracy were inherently one with the demands of a just and equal morality. We cannot now well use their vocabulary. Changes in knowledge have outlawed the significations of the words they commonly used. But in spite of the unsuitability of much of their language for present use, what they asserted was that self-governing institutions are the means by which human nature can secure its fullest realization in the greatest number of persons. The question of what is involved in self-governing methods is now much more complex. But for this very reason, the task of those who retain belief in democracy is to revive and maintain in full vigor the original conviction of the intrinsic moral nature of democracy, now stated in ways congruous with present conditions of culture. We have advanced far enough to say that democracy is a way of life. We have yet to realize that it is a way of personal life and one which provides a moral standard for personal conduct.

6.   Science and Free Culture

It is no longer possible to hold the simple faith of the Enlightenment that assured advance of science will produce free institutions by dispelling ignorance and superstition:—the sources of human servitude and the pillars of oppressive government. The progress of natural science has been even more rapid and extensive than could have been anticipated. But its technological application in mass production and distribution of goods has required concentration of capital; it has resulted in business corporations possessed of extensive legal rights and immunities; and, as is a commonplace, has created a vast and intricate set of new problems. It has put at the disposal of dictators means of controlling opinion and sentiment of a potency which reduces to a mere shadow all previous agencies at the command of despotic rulers. For negative censorship it has substituted means of propaganda of ideas and alleged information on a scale that reaches every individual, reiterated day after day by every organ of publicity and communication, old and new. In consequence, for practically the first time in human history, totalitarian states exist claiming to rest upon the active consent of the governed. While despotic governments are as old as political history, this particular phenomenon is as startlingly unexpected as it is powerful.

One of the earlier arguments for democracy is countered in the most disturbing way. Before the industrial revolution had made much headway it was a commonplace that oppressive governments had the support of only a relatively small class. Republican government, it was assumed, would have the broad support of the masses, so that the "people" who, as Rousseau expressed it, had been nothing would become everything. We are now told the contrary. Democracy is said to be but a numerical contrivance, resting upon shifting combinations of individuals who happen at a given time to make up a majority of voters. We are told that the moral consensus which exists only when there is unity of beliefs and aims, is conspicuously lacking in democracies, and is of the very essence of totalitarian states. The claim stands side by side with that of Marxist communists who say that since their views are inherently scientific, false opinions have no legitimate standing as against the authority of The Truth. But in a way the Fascist claim goes deeper since it pretends to extend below merely intellectual loyalties, to which science appeals, and lay hold of fundamental emotions and impulses.

There is an argument about science which so far has found comparatively little response in democratic countries, but which nevertheless puts a problem so basic that it will receive more and more attention as time goes by. It is said that the principles of laissez-faire individualism have governed the conduct of scientific inquiry; that the tastes and preferences of individual investigators have been allowed to regulate its course to such an extent that present intellectual confusion and moral chaos of the world exists because of tacit connivance of science with uncontrolled individualistic activity in industry.

The position is so extreme and goes so contrary to all we had come to believe that it is easily passed over as an aberration. But the view, because of its extreme character, may be taken to point to a genuine issue: just what are the social consequences of science? Are they not so important, because of technological applications, that the social interest is paramount over intellectual interest? Can the type of social control of industry urged by socialists be carried through without some kind of public regulation of the scientific investigations that are the source of the inventions determining the course of industry? And might not such regulation throttle the freedom of science? Those who say that the social effect of inventions (which exist only because of the findings of scientific inquiry) is so unsettling that the least which can be done is to declare a moratorium on science express the same problem with more moderation.

The claim is made in Russia that the direction taken by science has in the last hundred and fifty years been so determined by the interest of the dominant economic class, that science has been upon the whole an organ of bourgeois democracy:—not so consciously perhaps as in the case of government, the police and the army, but yet in substantial effect. Since it is impossible to draw any fixed line between the physical and the social sciences, and since the latter—both with respect to investigation and teaching—must be regulated in the interest of the politics of the new social order, it is impossible to allow the physical sciences to go their way apart without political regulation. Nazi Germany decrees what is scientific truth in anthropology regarding race, and Moscow determines that Mendelism is scientifically false, and dictates the course to be pursued by Genetics. Both countries look askance at the theory of Relativity, although on different grounds. Quite aside, however, from special cases, a general atmosphere of control of opinion cannot exist without reacting in pretty fundamental ways upon every form of intellectual activity—art too as well as science.

Even if we hold that extreme views are so extreme as to be distorted caricatures, there remains an actual problem. Can society, especially a democratic society, exist without a basic consensus and community of beliefs? If it cannot, can the required community be achieved without regulation of scientific pursuits exercised by a public authority in behalf of social unity?

In this connection the accusation of irresponsibility as to social consequences is brought against scientific men, and it is in this context that the underlying issue takes shape. It is argued (and some who take the position are themselves scientists) that the main directions of physical science during the past hundred years, increasingly so in the last half century, have been set, indirectly and directly, by the requirements of industry carried on for private profit. Consideration of the *problems* which have not received attention in comparison with those which have absorbed expenditure of intellectual energies will, it is said, prove the proposition.

Direct control has been exercised for the most part by governments. They have subsidized the kind of investigations that promise increased national power, either by promoting manufacturing and commerce as against other national states, or by fostering researches that strengthen military prowess. Indirect control has been exercised in subtler ways. The place of industry is so central in modern life that quite apart from questions handed directly over to scientific laboratories by industrial enterprises, it is psychologically impossible for men engaged in scientific research not to be most sensitive and most responsive to the *type* of

problems presented in practical effort to control natural energies;—which in the concrete means manufacturing and dis-
tributing goods. Moreover, a kind of positive halo surrounds scientific endeavors. For it has been held, not without grounds, that
general social—or at least national—welfare is thereby promoted. Germany led other countries in physical research; and it
was in Germany that scientific advances could be shown to have
contributed most directly to national strength and prestige. It
was thus possible for some intellectual observers, not particularly naïve, to hold up German universities as models to follow in
our own country.

It is not implied that personal economic interest has played
any important part in directing the researches of individual scientists. The contrary is notoriously the rule. But attention and
interest are not freely ranging searchlights that can be directed at
all parts of the natural universe with equal ease. They operate
within certain channels, and the general state of culture determines what and where the channels are. The "climate of opinion"
decides the direction taken by scientific activity as truly as physical climate decides what agricultural pursuits can be carried on.
Social imagination comes to have a certain tone and color; intellectual immunity in one direction and intellectual sensitivity in
other directions are the result. It has even been said, and with a
good deal of evidence in its support, that the prevailing mecha-
nistic creed of science during the nineteenth century was an indirect product of the importance assumed by the machine in industrial production, so that now, when machine-production is
giving way to power-production, basic scientific "concepts" are
also changing.

I referred above to the role of nationalism in deciding the direction taken by science. The striking instance is of course the
organization of scientific men for aid to a nation in time of war.
The instance brings to a head tendencies that are going on in less
overt and more unconscious ways pretty much all the time, even
in times of nominal peace. Increase of the scope of governmental
activities in all industrialized countries, going on for some years
at an accelerated pace, has reinforced the alliance between national interest and scientific inquiry. It is certainly arguable that
when the choice at hand is between regulation of science by private economic interests and by nationalist interest, the latter

should have preference. It may be inferred that the open control of science exercised in totalitarian states is but a culmination of tendencies that have been going on in more or less covert ways for some time—from which it follows that the problem presented extends beyond the borders of those particular states.

Strangely enough, at first sight, the demand for direct social control of scientific inquiries and conclusion is unwittingly reinforced by an attitude quite commonly taken by scientific men themselves. For it is commonly said and commonly believed that science is completely neutral and indifferent as to the ends and values which move men to act: that at most it only provides more efficient means for realization of ends that are and must be due to wants and desires completely independent of science. It is at this point that the present climate of opinion differs so widely from that which marked the optimistic faith of the Enlightenment; the faith that human science and freedom would advance hand in hand to usher in an era of indefinite human perfectibility.

That the popular esteem of science is largely due to the aid it has given to men for attainment of things they wanted independently of what they had learned from science is doubtless true. Russell has stated in a vivid way the sort of thing that has enabled science to displace beliefs that had previously been held: "The world ceased to believe that Joshua caused the sun to stand still, because Copernican astronomy was useful in navigation; it abandoned Aristotle's physics, because Galileo's theory of falling bodies made it possible to calculate the trajectory of a cannonball. It rejected the theory of the flood because geology is useful in mining and so on."[1] That the quotation expresses the sort of thing that gave the conclusions of the new science prestige and following at a time when it badly needed some outside aid in getting a hearing can hardly be doubted. As illustrative material it is especially impressive because of the enormous authority enjoyed by the doctrines of Aristotle and of the Church. If even in the case where all the advantage was on the side of old doctrines, the demonstrated serviceability of science gave it the victory, we can easily judge the enhancement of the esteem in which science was held in matters where it had no such powerful foe to contend with.

Quite apart from the antagonism to science displayed by en-

1. Bertrand Russell, *Power*, p. 138.

trenched institutional interests that had previously obtained a monopoly over beliefs in, say, astronomy, geology and some fields of history, history proves the existence of so much indifference on the part of mankind to the quality of its beliefs and such lethargy towards methods that disturb old beliefs, that we should be glad that the new science has had such powerful adventitious aid. But it leaves untouched the question as to whether scientific knowledge has power to modify the ends which men prize and strive to attain. Is it proved that the findings of science—the best authenticated knowledge we have—add only to our power to realize desires already in existence? Or is this view derived from some previous theory about the constitution of human nature? Can it be true that desires and knowledge exist in separate non-communicating compartments? Do the facts which can undoubtedly be cited as evidence, such as the use of scientific knowledge indifferently to heal disease and prolong human life and to provide the instruments for wholesale destruction of life, really prove the case? Or are they specially selected cases that support a doctrine that originated on other grounds than the evidence of facts? Is there such a complete separation of human ends from human beliefs as the theory assumes?

The shock given old ideas by the idea that knowledge is incapable of modifying the quality of desires (and hence cannot affect the formation of ends and purposes) is not of course in itself a ground for denying it is sound. It may be that the old view is totally false. Nevertheless, the point is worth discussion. We do not have to refer to the theory of Plato that knowledge, or what passes as knowledge, is the sole final determinant of men's ideas of the Good and hence of their actions. Nor is it needful to refer to Bacon's vision of the organization of scientific knowledge as the prospective foundation of future social policies directed exclusively to the advance of human well-being. The simple fact is that all the deliberately liberal and progressive movements of modern times have based themselves on the idea that action is determined by ideas, up to the time when Hume said that reason was and should be the "slave of the passions"; or, in contemporary language, of the emotions and desires. Hume's voice was a lonely one when he uttered the remark. The idea is now echoed and re-echoed from almost every quarter. The classic economic school made wants the prime motors of human action, reducing reason to a power of calculating the means best fitted to satisfy the wants. The first effect of biology upon psychology was to emphasize the primacy of appetites and instincts. Psychiatrists have enforced the same conclusion by showing that intellectual disturbances originate in emotional maladjustments, and by exhibiting the extent of dictation of belief by desire.

It is one thing, however, to recognize that earlier theories neglected the importance of emotions and habits as determinants of conduct and exaggerated that of ideas and reason. It is quite another thing to hold that ideas (especially those warranted by competent inquiry) and emotions (with needs and desires) exist in separate compartments so that no interaction between them exists. When the view is as baldly stated it strikes one as highly improbable that there can be any such complete separation in the constitution of human nature. And while the idea must be accepted if the evidence points that way, no matter into what plight human affairs are forever plunged, the implications of the doctrine of complete separation of desire and knowledge must be noted. The assumption that desires are rigidly fixed is not one on its face consistent with the history of man's progress from savagery through barbarism to even the present defective state of civilization. If knowledge, even of the most authenticated kind, cannot influence desires and aims, if it cannot determine what is of value and what is not, the future outlook as to formation of desires is depressing. Denial that they can be influenced by knowledge points emphatically to the non-rational and anti-rational forces that will form them. One alternative to the power of ideas is habit or custom, and then when the rule of sheer habit breaks down—as it has done at the present time—all that is left is competition on the part of various bodies and interests to decide which shall come out ahead in a struggle, carried on by intimidation, coercion, bribery, and all sorts of propaganda, to shape the desires which shall predominantly control the ends of human action. The prospect is a black one. It leads one to consider the possibility that Bacon, Locke, and the leaders of the Enlightenment—typified by the act of Condorcet, writing, while imprisoned and waiting for death, about the role of science in the future liberation of mankind—were after all quite aware of the actual influence of appetite, habit, and blind desire upon action, but were engaged in holding up another and better way as the alternative to follow in the future.

That the course they anticipated has not come to fruition is obvious without argument. Bacon's action in using his own knowledge as a servant of the Crown in strengthening Great Britain in a military way against other nations now seems more prophetic of what has happened than what he put down in words. The power over Nature which he expected to follow the advance of science has come to pass. But in contradiction to his expectations, it has been largely used to increase, instead of reduce, the power of Man over Man. Shall we conclude that the early prophets were totally and intrinsically wrong? Or shall we conclude that they immensely underestimated the obduracy of institutions and customs antedating the appearance of science on the scene in shaping desires in their image? Have events after all but accentuated the problem of discovering the means by which authenticated beliefs shall influence desires, the formation of ends, and thereby the course of events? Is it possible to admit the power of propaganda to shape ends and deny that of science?

Looked at from one angle, the question brings us back to our fundamental issue: the relation of culture and human nature. For the fact which is decisive in answering the question whether verified knowledge is or is not capable of shaping desires and ends (as well as means) is whether the desires that are effective in settling the course of action are innate and fixed, or are themselves the product of a certain culture. If the latter is the case, the practical issue reduces itself to this: Is it possible for the scientific attitude to become such a weighty and widespread constituent of culture that, through the medium of culture, it may shape human desires and purposes?

To state the question is a long way from ability to answer it. But it is something to have the issue before us in its actual instead of in its factitious form. The issue ceases to be the indeterminate one of the relation of knowledge and desires in the native psychological constitution of man—indeterminate, among other reasons, because it is disputable whether there is any such thing as the latter apart from native biological constitution. It becomes the determinate one of the institution of the kind of culture in which scientific method and scientific conclusions are integrally incorporated.

The problem stated in this way puts in a different light the esteem gained by science because of its serviceability. That there are individuals here and there who have been influenced to esteem science because of some obvious contribution to satisfaction of their merely personal desires may well be a fact. That there are groups similarly influenced must be admitted. But the reasons why men have been willing to accept conclusions derived from science in lieu of older ideas are not exclusively or even mainly those of direct personal and class benefit. Improvements in navigation and mining have become part of the state of culture. It is in this capacity they have tended to displace beliefs that were congenial to an earlier state of culture. By and large the same thing is true of the application of physics and chemistry in more effective satisfaction of wants and in creation of new wants. While their application to produce increased efficiency in carrying on war has doubtlessly recommended those sciences to persons like rulers and generals, who otherwise would have been indifferent, the mass of persons have been moved to an attitude of favorable esteem by what has happened in the arts of peace. The decisive factor would seem to be whether the arts of war or of peace are to be in the future the ones that will control culture, a question that involves the need of discovering why war is such an important constituent of present culture.

I should be on controversial ground if I held up as evidence the belief that the technologies, which are the practical correlates of scientific theories, have now reached a point in which they can be used to create an era of abundance instead of the deficit-economies that existed before natural science developed, and that with an era of abundance and security the causes of conflict would be reduced. It may be mentioned as a hypothetical illustration. The kind of serviceability which is capable of generating high esteem for science *may* possibly be serviceability for general and shared, or "social," welfare. If the economic regime were so changed that the resources of science were employed to maintain security for all, the present view about the limitation of science might fade away. I imagine there are not many who will deny that esteem for science, even when placed upon the ground of serviceability alone, is produced at least in part by an admixture of general with private serviceability. If there is a skeptic let him consider the contribution made by science both actually and still more potentially to agriculture, and the social consequences of the change in production of foods and raw materials, thereby effected.

The other side of the ledger is marked by such a debit entry as the following from the English chemist Soddy: "So far the pearls of science have been cast before swine, who have given us in return millionaires and slums, armaments and the desolation of war." The contrast is real. If its existence seems to support the doctrine that science only supplies means for more efficient execution of already existing desires and purposes, it is because it points to the division which exists in our culture. The war that mobilizes science for wholesale destruction mobilizes it, also, for support of life and for healing the wounded. The desires and ends involved proceed not from native and naked human nature but from modifications it has undergone in interaction with a complex of cultural factors of which science is indeed one, but one which produces social consequences only as it is affected by economic and political traditions and customs formed before its rise.

For in any case, the influence of science on both means and ends is not exercised directly upon individuals but indirectly through incorporation within culture. In this function and capacity it is that scientific beliefs have replaced earlier unscientific beliefs. The position stated at its worst is that science operates as a part of folklore, not just as science. Even when put in this way, attention is invited to differences in folklore and to differences of the consequences that are produced by different folklores. And when it is admitted that the folklore may be one of aggressive nationalism, where the consequences of science as part of the prevailing folklore is war of the present destructive scope, we at least have the advantage of clear knowledge as to the location of the problem.

We have been considering science as a body of conclusions. We have ignored science in its quality of an attitude embodied in habitual will to employ certain methods of observation, reflection, and test rather than others. When we look at science from this point of view, the significance of science as a constituent of culture takes on a new color. The great body of scientific inquirers would deny with indignation that they are actuated in *their* esteem for science by its material serviceability. If they use words sanctioned by long tradition, they say they are moved by love of the truth. If they use contemporary phraseology, less grandiloquent in sound but of equivalent meaning, they say they are moved by a controlling interest in inquiry, in discovery, in following where the evidence of discovered facts points. Above all they say that this kind of interest excludes interest in reaching any conclusion not warranted by evidence, no matter how personally congenial it may be.

In short, it is a fact that a certain group of men, perhaps relatively not very numerous, have a "disinterested" interest in scientific inquiry. This interest has developed a morale having its own distinctive features. Some of its obvious elements are willingness to hold belief in suspense, ability to doubt until evidence is obtained; willingness to go where evidence points instead of putting first a personally preferred conclusion; ability to hold ideas in solution and use them as hypotheses to be tested instead of as dogmas to be asserted; and (possibly the most distinctive of all) enjoyment of new fields for inquiry and of new problems.

Every one of these traits goes contrary to some human impulse that is naturally strong. Uncertainty is disagreeable to most persons; suspense is so hard to endure that assured expectation of an unfortunate outcome is usually preferred to a long-continued state of doubt. "Wishful thinking" is a comparatively modern phrase; but men upon the whole have usually believed what they wanted to believe, except as very convincing evidence made it impossible. Apart from a scientific attitude, guesses, with persons left to themselves, tend to become opinions and opinions dogmas. To hold theories and principles in solution, awaiting confirmation, goes contrary to the grain. Even today questioning a statement made by a person is often taken by him as a reflection upon his integrity, and is resented. For many millennia opposition to views widely held in a community was intolerable. It called down the wrath of the deities who are in charge of the group. Fear of the unknown, fear of change and novelty, tended, at all times before the rise of scientific attitude, to drive men into rigidity of beliefs and habits; they entered upon unaccustomed lines of behavior—even in matters of minor moment—with qualms which exacted rites of expiation. Exceptions to accepted rules have either been ignored or systematically explained away when they were too conspicuous to ignore. Baconian idols of the tribe, the cave, the theater, and den have caused men to rush to conclusions, and then to use all their powers to defend from criticism and change the conclusions arrived at. The connection of common law with custom and its resistance to change are familiar facts. Even religious beliefs and rites which were at first more or less heretical deviations harden into modes of action it is impious to question, after once they have become part of the habits of a group.

If I mention such familiar considerations it is in part to suggest that we may well be grateful that science has had undeniable social serviceability, and that to some extent and in some places strong obstructions to adoption of changed beliefs have been overcome. But the chief reason for calling attention to them is the proof they furnish that in some persons and to some degree science has already created a new morale—which is equivalent to the creation of new desires and new ends. The existence of the scientific attitude and spirit, even upon a limited scale, is proof that science is capable of developing a distinctive type of disposition and purpose: a type that goes far beyond provision of more effective means for realizing desires which exist independently of any effect of science.

It is not becoming, to put it moderately, for those who are themselves animated by the scientific morale to assert that other persons are incapable of coming into possession of it and being moved by it.

Such an attitude is saved from being professional snobbery only when it is the result of sheer thoughtlessness. When one and the same representative of the intellectual class denounces any view that attaches inherent importance to the consequences of science, claiming the view is false to the spirit of science—and also holds that it is impossible for science to do anything to affect desires and ends, the inconsistency demands explanation.

A situation in which the fundamental dispositions and ends of a few are influenced by science while that of most persons and most groups is not so influenced proves that the issue is cultural. The difference sets a social problem: what are the causes for the existence of this great gap, especially since it has such serious consequences? If it is possible for persons to have their beliefs formed on the ground of evidence, procured by systematic and competent inquiry, nothing can be more disastrous socially than that the great majority of persons should have them formed by habit, accidents of circumstance, propaganda, personal and class bias. The existence, even on a relatively narrow scale, of a morale of fairmindedness, intellectual integrity, of will to subordinate personal preference to ascertained facts and to share with others what is found out, instead of using it for personal gain, is a challenge of the most searching kind. Why don't a great many more persons have this attitude?

The answer given to this challenge is bound up with the fate of democracy. The spread of literacy, the immense extension of the influence of the press in books, newspapers, periodicals, make the issue peculiarly urgent for a democracy. The very agencies that a century and a half ago were looked upon as those that were sure to advance the cause of democratic freedom, are those which now make it possible to create pseudo-public opinion and to undermine democracy from within. Callousness due to continuous reiteration may produce a certain immunity to the grosser kinds of propaganda. But in the long run negative measures afford no assurance. While it would be absurd to believe it desirable or possible for every one to become a scientist when science is defined from the side of subject matter, the future of democracy is allied with spread of the scientific attitude. It is the sole guarantee against wholesale misleading by propaganda. More important still, it is the only assurance of the possibility of a public opinion intelligent enough to meet present social problems.

To become aware of the problem is a condition of taking steps toward its solution. The problem is in part economic. The nature of control of the means of publicity enters directly; sheer financial control is not a favorable sign. The democratic belief in free speech, free press and free assembly is one of the things that exposes democratic institutions to attack. For representatives of totalitarian states, who are the first to deny such freedom when they are in power, shrewdly employ it in a democratic country to destroy the foundations of democracy. Backed with the necessary financial means, they are capable of carrying on a work of continuous sapping and mining. More dangerous, perhaps, in the end is the fact that all economic conditions tending toward centralization and concentration of the means of production and distribution affect the public press, whether individuals so desire or not. The causes which require large corporate capital to carry on modern business, naturally influence the publishing business.

The problem is also an educative one. A book instead of a paragraph could be given to this aspect of the topic. That the schools have mostly been given to imparting information ready-made, along with teaching the tools of literacy, cannot be denied. The methods used in acquiring such information are not those which develop skill in inquiry and in test of opinions. On the contrary, they are positively hostile to it. They tend to dull native curiosity, and to load powers of observation and experimentation with such a mass of unrelated material that they do not operate as effectively as they do in many an illiterate person. The problem of the common schools in a democracy has reached only its first stage when they are provided for everybody. Until what shall be taught and how it is taught is settled upon the basis of formation of the scientific attitude, the so-called educational work of schools is a dangerously hit-or-miss affair as far as democracy is concerned.

The problem—as was suggested earlier—is also one of art. It is difficult to write briefly on this aspect of the question without giving rise to false impressions. For of late there has been an active campaign, carried on in the name of the social function of art, for using the arts, the plastic arts as well as literature, in propaganda for special views which are dogmatically asserted to be socially necessary. In consequence, any reference to the topic may seem to have a flavor of commendation of something of the same kind, only exercised by way of a counter-campaign in behalf of democratic ideas. The point is different. It is a reminder that ideas are effective not as bare ideas but as they have imaginative content and emotional appeal. I have alluded to the extensive reaction that has set in against the earlier over-simplified rationalism. The reaction tended to go to an opposite extreme. In emphasizing the role of wants, impulse, habit, and emotion, it often denied any efficacy whatever to ideas, to intelligence. The problem is that of effecting the union of ideas and knowledge with the non-rational factors in the human make-up. Art is the name given to all the agencies by which this union is effected.

The problem is also a moral and religious one. That religions have operated most effectively in alliance with the fine arts was indicated earlier. Yet the historic influence of religions has often been to magnify doctrines that are not subject to critical inquiry and test. Their cumulative effect in producing habits of mind at odds with the attitudes required for maintenance of democracy is probably much greater than is usually recognized. Shrewd observers have said that one factor in the relatively easy victory of totalitarianism in Germany was the void left by decay of former theological beliefs. Those who had lost one external authority upon which they had depended were ready to turn to another one which was closer and more tangible.

To say that the issue is a moral one is to say that in the end it comes back to personal choice and action. From one point of view everything which has been said is a laboring of the commonplace that democratic government is a function of public opinion and public sentiment. But identification of its formation in the democratic direction with democratic extension of the scientific morale till it is part of the ordinary equipment of the ordinary individual indicates the issue is a moral one. It is individual persons who need to have this attitude substituted for pride and prejudice, for class and personal interest, for beliefs made dear by custom and early emotional associations. It is only by the choice and the active endeavor of many individuals that this result can be effected.

A former president of the United States once made a political stir by saying that "Public office is a public trust." The saying was a truism although one that needed emphasis. That possession of knowledge and special skill in intellectual methods is a public trust has not become a truism even in words. Scientific morale has developed in some persons to a point where it is a matter of course that what is found out is communicated to other persons who are also engaged in specialized research. But it has not developed to the point where wider responsibility for communication is acknowledged. Circumstances which have attended the historic growth of modern science explain why this is so, although they do not justify its continuance. Internal and external circumstances have brought about a social seclusion of science which from a certain standpoint is analogous to an earlier monastic seclusion.

The external circumstance was the opposition scientific men had to overcome before it was possible for them to carry on their work free from dictation or persecution. The internal circumstance was in part the need for extreme specialization of inquiries which necessarily accompanied the novelty of the new method; in part, it was a self-protective policy for maintaining the purity of a new, still immature and struggling attitude from contamination that proceeded from taking sides in practical affairs. This attitude had the blessing of the old and ingrained tradition of the "purity" of science as an exclusively theoretical subject; a subject aloof from practice, since reason and theory were so high above practice, which was, according to tradition, only material and utilitarian. The danger of loss of the impartiality of the scientific spirit through affiliation with some partisan and partial interest seemed to give significance to the established tradition about "purity," which, like traditional feminine chastity, needed all kinds of external safeguards to hedge it about. The need is not that scientific men become crusaders in special practical causes. Just as the problem with art is to unite the inherent integrity of the artist with imaginative and emotional appeal of ideas, so the present need is recognition by scientific men of social responsibility for contagious diffusion of the scientific attitude: a task not to be accomplished without abandoning once for all the belief that science is set apart from all other social interests as if possessed of a peculiar holiness.

Extension of the qualities that make up the scientific attitude is quite a different matter than dissemination of the results of physics, chemistry, biology and astronomy, valuable as the latter may be. The difference is the reason why the issue is a moral one. The question of whether science is capable of influencing the formation of ends for which men strive or is limited to increasing power of realizing those which are formed independently of it is the question whether science has intrinsic moral potentiality. Historically, the position that science is devoid of moral quality has been held by theologians and their metaphysical allies. For the position points unmistakably to the necessity for recourse to some other source of moral guidance. That a similar position is now taken in the name of science is either a sign of a confusion that permeates all aspects of culture, or is an omen of ill for democracy. If control of conduct amounts to conflict of desires with no possibility of determination of desire and purpose by scientifically warranted beliefs, then the practical alternative is competition and conflict between unintelligent forces for control of desire. The conclusion is so extreme as to suggest that denial in the name of science of the existence of any such things as moral facts may mark a transitional stage thoughtlessly taken to be final. It is quite true that science cannot affect moral values, ends, rules, principles as these were once thought of and believed in, namely, prior to the rise of science. But to say that there are no such things as moral facts because desires control formation and valuation of ends is in truth but to point to desires and interests as themselves moral facts requiring control by intelligence equipped with knowledge. Science through its physical technological consequences is now determining the relations which human beings, severally and in groups, sustain to one another. If it is incapable of developing moral techniques which will also determine these relations, the split in modern culture goes so deep that not only democracy but all civilized values are doomed. Such at least is the problem. A culture which permits science to destroy traditional values but which distrusts its power to create new ones is a culture which is destroying itself. War is a symptom as well as a cause of the inner division.

7. Democracy and America

I make no apology for linking what is said in this chapter with the name of Thomas Jefferson. For he was the first modern to state in human terms the principles of democracy. Were I to make an apology, it would be that in the past I have concerned myself unduly, if a comparison has to be made, with the English writers who have attempted to state the ideals of self-governing communities and the methods appropriate to their realization. If I now prefer to refer to Jefferson it is not, I hope, because of American provincialism, even though I believe that only one who was attached to American soil and who took a consciously alert part in the struggles of the country to attain its independence, could possibly have stated as thoroughly and intimately as did Jefferson the aims embodied in the American tradition: "the definitions and axioms of a free government," as Lincoln called them. Nor is the chief reason for going to him, rather than to Locke or Bentham or Mill, his greater sobriety of judgment due to that constant tempering of theory with practical experience which also kept his democratic doctrine within human bounds.

The chief reason is that Jefferson's formulation is moral through and through: in its foundations, its methods, its ends. The heart of his faith is expressed in his words "Nothing is unchangeable but inherent and inalienable rights of man." The words in which he stated the moral basis of free institutions have gone out of vogue. We repeat the opening words of the Declaration of Independence, but unless we translate them they are couched in a language that, even when it comes readily to our tongue, does not penetrate today to the brain. He wrote: "These truths are self-evident: that all men are created equal; that they are endowed by their Creator with inherent and unalienable rights; that among these are life, liberty and the pursuit of happiness." Today we are wary of anything purporting to be self-evident truths; we are not given to associating politics with the plans of the Creator; the doctrine of natural rights which governed his style of expression has been weakened by historic and by philosophic criticism.

To put ourselves in touch with Jefferson's position we have therefore to translate the word "natural" into *moral*. Jefferson was under the influence of the Deism of his time. Nature and the plans of a benevolent and wise Creator were never far apart in his reflections. But his fundamental beliefs remain unchanged in substance if we forget all special associations with the word *Nature* and speak instead of ideal aims and values to be realized— aims which, although ideal, are not located in the clouds but are backed by something deep and indestructible in the needs and demands of humankind.

Were I to try to connect in any detail what I have to say with the details of Jefferson's speeches and letters—he wrote no theoretical treatises—I should probably seem to be engaged in a partisan undertaking; I should at times be compelled to indulge in verbal exegesis so as to attribute to him ideas not present in his mind. Nevertheless, there are three points contained in what has to be said about American democracy that I shall here explicitly connect with his name. In the first place, in the quotation made, it was the *ends* of democracy, the rights of *man*—not of men in the plural—which are unchangeable. It was not the forms and mechanisms through which inherent moral claims are realized that are to persist without change. Professed Jeffersonians have often not even followed the words of the one whose disciples they say they are, much less his spirit. For he said: "I know that laws and institutions must go hand in hand with the progress of the human mind. . . . As new discoveries are made, new truths disclosed, and manners and opinions change with the change of circumstances, institutions must change also and keep pace with the times. We might as well require a man to wear the coat which fitted him when a boy, as civilized society to remain ever under the regime of their barbarous ancestors."

Because of the last sentence his idea might be interpreted to be a justification of the particular change in government he was championing against earlier institutions. But he goes on to say: "Each generation has a right to choose for itself the form of government it believes the most promotive of its own happiness." Hence he also said: "The idea that institutions established for the use of a nation cannot be touched or modified, even to make them answer their end . . . may perhaps be a salutary provision against the abuses of a monarch, but is most absurd against the nation itself." "A generation holds all the rights and powers their predecessors once held and may change their laws and institutions to suit themselves." He engaged in certain calculations based on Buffon, more ingenious than convincing, to settle upon a period of eighteen years and eight months that fixed the natural span of the life of a generation; thereby indicating the frequency with which it is desirable to overhaul "laws and institutions" to bring them into accord with "new discoveries, new truths, change of manners and opinions." The word *culture* is not used; Jefferson's statement would have been weakened by its use. But it is not only professed followers of Jefferson who have failed to act upon his teaching. It is true of all of us so far as we have set undue store by established mechanisms. The most flagrantly obvious violation of Jefferson's democratic point of view is found in the idolatry of the Constitution as it stands that has been sedulously cultivated. But it goes beyond this instance. As believers in democracy we have not only the right but the duty to question existing mechanisms of, say, suffrage and to inquire whether some functional organization would not serve to formulate and manifest public opinion better than the existing methods. It is not irrelevant to the point that a score of passages could be cited in which Jefferson refers to the American Government as an *experiment*.

The second point of which I would speak is closely bound up with an issue which has become controversial and partisan, namely, states rights versus federal power. There is no question of where Jefferson stood on that issue, nor as to his fear in general of governmental encroachment on liberty—inevitable in his case, since it was the cause of the Rebellion against British domination and was also the ground of his struggle against Hamiltonianism. But any one who stops with this particular aspect of Jefferson's doctrine misses an underlying principle of utmost importance. For while he stood for state action as a barrier against excessive power at Washington, and while on the *practical side* his concern with it was most direct, in his theoretical writings chief importance is attached to local self-governing units on something like the New England town-meeting plan. His project for general political organization on the basis of small units, small enough so that all its members could have direct communication with one another and take care of all community affairs was never acted upon. It never received much attention in the press of immediate practical problems.

But without forcing the significance of this plan, we may find in it an indication of one of the most serious of present problems regarding democracy. I spoke earlier of the way in which individuals at present find themselves in the grip of immense forces whose workings and consequences they have no power of affecting. The situation calls emphatic attention to the need for face-to-face associations, whose interactions with one another may offset if not control the dread impersonality of the sweep of present forces. There is a difference between a society, in the sense of an association, and a community. Electrons, atoms and molecules are in association with one another. Nothing exists in isolation anywhere throughout nature. Natural associations are conditions for the existence of a community, but a community adds the function of communication in which emotions and ideas are shared as well as joint undertakings engaged in. Economic forces have immensely widened the scope of associational activities. But it has done so largely at the expense of the intimacy and directness of communal group interests and activities. The American habit of "joining" is a tribute to the reality of the problem but has not gone far in solving it. The power of the rabblerouser, especially in the totalitarian direction, is mainly due to his power to create a factitious sense of direct union and communal solidarity—if only by arousing the emotion of common intolerance and hate.

I venture to quote words written some years ago: "Evils which are uncritically and indiscriminately laid at the door of industrialism and democracy might, with greater intelligence, be referred to the dislocation and unsettlement of local communities. Vital and thorough attachments are bred only in the intimacy of an intercourse which is of necessity restricted in range. . . . Is it possible to restore the reality of the less communal organizations and to penetrate and saturate their members with a sense of local community life? . . . Democracy must begin at home, and its home is the neighborly community." [1] On account of the vast ex-

1. *The Public and Its Problems*, pp. 212–13 [*Later Works* 2:367–68].

tension of the field of association, produced by elimination of distance and lengthening of temporal spans, it is obvious that social agencies, political and non-political, cannot be confined to localities. But the problem of harmonious adjustment between extensive activities, precluding direct contacts, and the intensive activities of community intercourse is a pressing one for democracy. It involves even more than apprenticeship in the practical processes of self-government, important as that is, which Jefferson had in mind. It involves development of local agencies of communication and cooperation, creating stable loyal attachments, to militate against the centrifugal forces of present culture, while at the same time they are of a kind to respond flexibly to the demands of the larger unseen and indefinite public. To a very considerable extent, groups having a functional basis will probably have to replace those based on physical contiguity. In the family both factors combine.

The third point of which I would make express mention as to Jefferson and democracy has to do with his ideas about property. It would be absurd to hold that his personal views were "radical" beyond fear of concentrated wealth and a positive desire for general distribution of wealth without great extremes in either direction. However, it is sometimes suggested that his phrase "pursuit of happiness" stood for economic activity, so that life, liberty, and property were the rights he thought organized society should maintain. But just here is where he broke most completely with Locke. In connection with property, especially property in land, he makes his most positive statements about the inability of any generation to bind its successors. Jefferson held that property rights are created by the "social pact" instead of representing inherent individual moral claims which government is morally bound to maintain.

The right to pursue happiness stood with Jefferson for nothing less than the claim of every human being to choose his own career and to act upon his own choice and judgment free from restraints and constraints imposed by the arbitrary will of other human beings—whether these others are officials of government, of whom Jefferson was especially afraid, or are persons whose command of capital and control of the opportunities for engaging in useful work limits the ability of others to "pursue happiness." The Jeffersonian principle of equality of rights without special favor to any one justifies giving supremacy to personal rights when they come into conflict with property rights. While his views are properly enough cited against ill-considered attacks upon the economic relations that exist at a given time, it is sheer perversion to hold that there is anything in Jeffersonian democracy that forbids political action to bring about equalization of economic conditions in order that the equal right of all to free choice and free action be maintained.

I have referred with some particularity to Jefferson's ideas upon special points because of the proof they afford that the source of the American democratic tradition is moral—not technical, abstract, narrowly political nor materially utilitarian. It is moral because based on faith in the ability of human nature to achieve freedom for individuals accompanied with respect and regard for other persons and with social stability built on cohesion instead of coercion. Since the tradition is a moral one, attacks upon it, however they are made, wherever they come from, from within or from without, involve moral issues and can be settled only upon moral grounds. In as far as the democratic ideal has undergone eclipse among us, the obscuration is moral in source and effect. The dimming is both a product and a manifestation of the confusion that accompanies transition from an old order to a new one for the arrival of the latter was heralded only as conditions plunged it into an economic regime so novel that there was no adequate preparation for it and which dislocated the established relations of persons with one another.

Nothing is gained by attempts to minimize the novelty of the democratic order, nor the scope of the change it requires in old and long cherished traditions. We have not even as yet a common and accepted vocabulary in which to set forth the order of moral values involved in realization of democracy. The language of Natural Law was once all but universal in educated Christendom. The conditions which gave it force disappeared. Then there was an appeal to natural rights, supposed by some to centre in isolated individuals—although not in the original American formulation. At present, appeal to the individual is dulled by our inability to locate the individual with any assurance. While we are compelled to note that his freedom can be maintained only through the working together toward a single end of a large number of different and complex factors, we do not know how to coordinate them on the basis of voluntary purpose.

The intimate association that was held to exist between individualism and business activity for private profit gave, on one side, a distorted meaning to individualism. Then the weakening, even among persons who nominally retain older theological beliefs, of the imaginative ideas and emotions connected with the sanctity of the individual, disturbed democratic individualism on the positive moral side. The moving energy once associated with things called spiritual has lessened; we use the word *ideal* reluctantly, and have difficulty in giving the word *moral* much force beyond, say, a limited field of mutually kindly relations among individuals. That such a syllogism as the following once had a vital meaning to a man of affairs like Jefferson today seems almost incredible: "Man was created for social intercourse, but social intercourse cannot be maintained without a sense of justice; then man must have been created with a sense of justice."

Even if we have an abiding faith in democracy, we are not likely to express it as Jefferson expressed his faith: "I have no fear but that the result of our experiment will be that men may be trusted to govern themselves without a master. Could the contrary of this be proved, I should conclude either there is no God or that he is a malevolent being." The belief of Jefferson that the sole legitimate object of government among men "is to secure the greatest degree of happiness possible to the general mass of those associated under it" was connected with his belief that Nature—or God—benevolent in intent, had created men for happiness on condition they attained knowledge of natural order and observed the demands of that knowledge in their actions. The obsolescence of the language for many persons makes it the more imperative for all who would maintain and advance the ideals of democracy to face the issue of the moral ground of political institutions and the moral principles by which men acting together may attain freedom of individuals which will amount to fraternal associations with one another. The weaker our faith in Nature, in its laws and rights and its benevolent intentions for human welfare, the more urgent is the need for a faith based on ideas that are now intellectually credible and that are consonant with present economic conditions, which will inspire and direct action with something of the ardor once attached to things religious.

Human power over the physical energies of nature has immensely increased. In moral ideal, power of man over physical nature should be employed to reduce, to eliminate progressively, the power of man over man. By what means shall we prevent its use to effect new, more subtle, more powerful agencies of subjection of men to other men? Both the issue of war or peace between nations, and the future of economic relations for years and generations to come in contribution either to human freedom or human subjection are involved. An increase of power undreamed of a century ago, one to whose further increase no limits can be put as long as scientific inquiry goes on, is an established fact. The thing still uncertain is what we are going to do with it. That it is power signifies of itself it is electrical, thermic, chemical. What will be done with it is a moral issue.

Physical interdependence has increased beyond anything that could have been foreseen. Division of labor in industry was anticipated and was looked forward to with satisfaction. But it is relatively the least weighty phase of the present situation. The career of individuals, their lives and security as well as prosperity is now affected by events on the other side of the world. The forces back of these events he cannot touch or influence—save perhaps by joining in a war of nations against nations. For we seem to live in a world in which nations try to deal with the problems created by the new situation by drawing more and more into themselves, by more and more extreme assertions of independent nationalist sovereignty, while everything they do in the direction of autarchy leads to ever closer mixture with other nations—but in war.

War under existing conditions compels nations, even those professedly the most democratic, to turn authoritarian and totalitarian as the World War of 1914–18 resulted in Fascist totalitarianism in non-democratic Italy and Germany and in Bolshevist totalitarianism in non-democratic Russia, and promoted political, economic and intellectual reaction in this country. The necessity of transforming physical interdependence into moral—into human—interdependence is part of the democratic problem: and yet war is said even now to be the path of salvation for democratic countries!

Individuals can find the security and protection that are prerequisites for freedom only in association with others—and then the organization these associations take on, as a measure of securing their efficiency, limits the freedom of those who have entered into them. The importance of organization has increased so much in the last hundred years that the word is now quite commonly used as a synonym for association and society. Since at the very best organization is but the mechanism through which association operates, the identification is evidence of the extent in which a servant has become a master; in which means have usurped the place of the end for which they are called into existence. The predicament is that individuality demands association to develop and sustain it and association requires arrangement and coordination of its elements, or organization—since otherwise it is formless and void of power. But we have now a kind of molluscan organization, soft individuals within and a hard constrictive shell without. Individuals voluntarily enter associations which have become practically nothing but organizations; and then conditions under which they act take control of what they do whether they want it or not.

Persons acutely aware of the dangers of regimentation when it is imposed by government remain oblivious of the millions of persons whose behavior is regimented by an economic system through whose intervention alone they obtain a livelihood. The contradiction is the more striking because the new organizations were for the most part created in the name of freedom, and, at least at the outset, by exercise of voluntary choice. But the kind of working-together which has resulted is too much like that of the parts of a machine to represent a cooperation which expresses freedom and also contributes to it. No small part of the democratic problem is to achieve associations whose ordering of parts provides the strength that comes from stability, while they promote flexibility of response to change.

Lastly, in this brief survey, there is the problem of the relation of human nature and physical nature. The ancient world solved the problem, in abstract philosophical theory, by endowing all nature, in its cosmic scope, with the moral qualities of the highest and most ideal worth in humanity. The theology and rites of the Church gave this abstract theory direct significance in the lives of the peoples of the western world. For it provided practical agencies by means of which the operation of the power creating and maintaining the universe were supposed to come to the support of individuals in this world and the next. The rise of physical science rendered an ever increasing number of men skeptical of the intellectual foundation provided by the old theory. The unsettlement, going by the name of the conflict of science and religion, proves the existence of the division in the foundations upon which our culture rests, between ideas in the form of knowledge and ideas that are emotional and imaginative and that directly actuate conduct.

This disturbance on the moral side has been enormously aggravated by those who are remote from the unsettlement due to intellectual causes. It comes home to everyone by the effects of the practical application of the new physical science. For all the physical features of the present regime of production and distribution of goods and services are products of the new physical science, while the distinctively *human* consequences of science are still determined by habits and beliefs established before its origin. That democracy should not as yet have succeeded in healing the breach is no cause for discouragement: provided there is effected a union of human possibilities and ideals with the spirit and methods of science on one side and with the workings of the economic system on the other side. For a considerable period laissez-faire individualism prevented the problem from being even seen. It treated the new economic movement as if it were simply an expression of forces that were fundamental in the human constitution but were only recently released for free operation. It failed to see that the great expansion which was occurring was in fact due to release of *physical* energies; that as far as human action and human freedom is concerned, a problem, not a solution, was thereby instituted: the problem, namely, of management and direction of the new physical energies so they would contribute to realization of human possibilities.

The reaction that was created by the inevitable collapse of a movement that failed so disastrously in grasp of the problem has had diverse results, the diversity of which is part of the present confused state of our lives. Production of the material means of a secure and free life has been indefinitely increased and at an accelerated rate. It is not surprising that there is a large group which attributes the gains which have accrued, actually and potentially, to the economic regime under which they have occurred—instead of to the scientific knowledge which is the source of physical control of natural energies. The group is large. It is composed not only of the immediate beneficiaries of the system but also of the much larger number who hope that they, or at least their children, are to have full share in its benefits. Because of the opportunities furnished by free land, large unused natural resources and the absence of fixed class differences (which survive in European countries in spite of legal abolition of feudalism), this group is particularly large in this country. It is represented by those who point to the higher standard of living in this country and by those who have responded to the greater opportunities for advancement this country has afforded to them. In short, this group, in both categories of its constituents, is impressed by actual gains that have come about. They have a kind of blind and touching faith that improvement is going to continue in some more or less automatic way until it includes them and their offspring.

Then there is a much smaller group who are as sensitive, perhaps more so, to the immense possibilities represented by the physical means now potentially at our command, but who are acutely aware of our failure to realize them; who see instead the miseries, cruelties, oppressions and frustrations which exist. The weakness of this group has been that it has also failed to realize the involvement of the new scientific method in producing the existing state of affairs, and the need for its further extensive and unremitting application to determine analytically—in detail—the causes of present ills, and to project means for their elimination. In social affairs, the wholesale mental attitude that has been referred to persists with little change. It leads to formation of ambitious and sweeping beliefs and policies. The human *ideal* is indeed comprehensive. As a standpoint from which to view existing conditions and judge the direction change should take, it cannot be too inclusive. But the problem of production of change is one of infinite attention to means; and means can be determined only by definite analysis of the conditions of each problem as it presents itself. Health is a comprehensive, a "sweeping" ideal. But progress toward it has been made in the degree in which recourse to panaceas has been abandoned and inquiry has been directed to determinate disturbances and means for dealing with them. The group is represented at its extreme by those who believe there is a necessary historical law which governs the course of events so that all that is needed is deliberate acting in accord with it. The law by which class conflict produces by its own dialectic its complete opposite becomes then the supreme and sole regulator for determining policies and methods of action.

That more adequate knowledge of human nature is demanded if the release of physical powers is to serve human ends is undeniable. But it is a mistake to suppose that this knowledge of itself enables us to control human energies as physical science has enabled us to control physical energies. It suffers from the fallacy into which those have fallen who have supposed that physical energies put at our disposal by science are sure to produce human progress and prosperity. A more adequate science of human nature might conceivably only multiply the agencies by which some human beings manipulate other human beings for their own advantage. Failure to take account of the moral phase of the problem, the question of values and ends, marks, although from the opposite pole, a relapse into the fallacy of the theorists of a century ago who assumed that "free"— that is to say, politically unrestrained—manifestation of human wants and impulses would tend to bring about social prosperity, progress, and harmony. It is a counterpart fallacy to the Marxist notion that there is an economic or "materialistic," dialectic of history by which a certain desirable (and in that sense moral) end will be brought about with no intervention of choice of values and effort to realize them. As I wrote some years ago, "the assimilation of human science to physical science represents only another form of absolutistic logic, a kind of physical absolutism."

Social events will continue, in any case, to be products of interaction of human nature with cultural conditions. Hence the primary and fundamental question will always be what sort of social results we supremely want. Improved science of human nature would put at our disposal means, now lacking, for defining the problem and working effectively for its solution. But save as it should reinforce respect for the morale of science, and thereby extend and deepen the incorporation of the attitudes which form the method of science into the disposition of individuals, it might add a complication similar to that introduced by improved physical science. Anything that obscures the fundamentally moral nature of the social problem is harmful, no matter whether it proceeds from the side of physical or of psychological theory. Any doctrine that eliminates or even obscures the function of choice of values and enlistment of desires and emotions in behalf of those chosen weakens personal responsibility for judgment and for action. It thus helps create the attitudes that welcome and support the totalitarian state.

I have stated in bare outline some of the outstanding phases of the problem of culture in the service of democratic freedom. Difficulties and obstacles have been emphasized. This emphasis is a result of the fact that a *problem* is presented. Emphasis upon the problem is due to belief that many weaknesses which events have disclosed are connected with failure to see the immensity of the task involved in setting mankind upon the democratic road. That with a background of millennia of non-democratic societies behind them, the earlier advocates of democracy tremendously simplified the issue is natural. For a time the simplification was an undoubted asset. Too long continued it became a liability.

Recognition of the scope and depth of the problem is neither depressing nor discouraging when the democratic movement is placed in historic perspective. The ideas by which it formulated itself have a long history behind them. We can trace their source in Hellenic humanism and in Christian beliefs; and we can also find recurrent efforts to realize this or that special aspect of these ideas in some special struggle against a particular form of oppression. By proper selection and arrangement, we can even make out a case for the idea that all past history has been a movement, at first unconscious and then conscious, to attain freedom. A more sober view of history discloses that it took a very fortunate conjunction of events to bring about the rapid spread and seemingly complete victory of democracy during the nineteenth century. The conclusion to be drawn is not the depressing one that it is now in danger of destruction because of an unfavorable conjunction of events. The conclusion is that what was won in a more or less external and accidental manner must now be achieved and sustained by deliberate and intelligent endeavor.

The contrast thus suggested calls attention to the fact that underlying persistent attitudes of human beings were formed by traditions, customs, institutions, which existed when there was no democracy—when in fact democratic ideas and aspirations

tended to be strangled at birth. Persistence of these basic dispositions accounts, on one side, for the sudden attack upon democracy; it is a reversion to old emotional and intellectual habits; or
rather it is not so much a reversion as it is a manifestation of attitudes that have been there all the time but have been more or less
covered up. Their persistence also explains the depth and range
of the present problem. The struggle for democracy has to be
maintained on as many fronts as culture has aspects: political,
economic, international, educational, scientific and artistic, religious. The fact that we now have to accomplish of set purpose
what in an earlier period was more or less a gift of grace renders
the problem a moral one to be worked out on moral grounds.

Part of the fortunate conjunction of circumstances with respect to us who live here in the United States consists, as has been
indicated, of the fact that our forefathers found themselves in a
new land. The shock of physical dislocation effected a very considerable modification of old attitudes. Habits of thought and
feeling which were the products of long centuries of accultura-
tion were loosened. Less entrenched dispositions dropped off.
The task of forming new institutions was thereby rendered immensely easier. The readjustment thus effected has been a chief
factor in creating a general attitude of adaptability that has enabled us, save for the Civil War, to meet change with a minimum
of external conflict and, in spite of an heritage of violence, with
good nature. It is because of such consequences that the geo-
graphical New World may become a New World in a human
sense. But, all the more on this account, the situation is such that
most of the things about which we have been complacent and
self-congratulatory now have to be won by thought and effort,
instead of being results of evolution of a manifest destiny.

In the present state of affairs, a conflict of the moral Old and
New Worlds is the essence of the struggle for democracy. It is not
a question for us of isolationism, although the physical factors
which make possible physical isolation from the warring ambitions of Europe are a factor to be cherished in an emergency. The
conflict is not one waged with arms, although the question
whether we again take up arms on European battlefields for ends
that are foreign to the ends to which this country is dedicated
will have weight in deciding whether we win or lose our own
battle on our own ground. It is possible to stay out for reasons

that have nothing to do with the maintenance of democracy, and a good deal to do with pecuniary profit, just as it is possible to be deluded into participation in the name of fighting for democracy. The conflict as it concerns the democracy to which our history commits us is *within* our own institutions and attitudes. It can be won only by extending the application of democratic methods, methods of consultation, persuasion, negotiation, communication, cooperative intelligence, in the task of making our own politics, industry, education, our culture generally, a servant and an evolving manifestation of democratic ideas. Resort to military force is a first sure sign that we are giving up the struggle for the democratic way of life, and that the Old World has conquered morally as well as geographically—succeeding in imposing upon us its ideals and methods.

If there is one conclusion to which human experience unmistakably points it is that democratic ends demand democratic methods for their realization. Authoritarian methods now offer themselves to us in new guises. They come to us claiming to serve the ultimate ends of freedom and equity in a classless society. Or they recommend adoption of a totalitarian regime in order to fight totalitarianism. In whatever form they offer themselves, they owe their seductive power to their claim to serve ideal ends. Our first defense is to realize that democracy can be served only by the slow day by day adoption and contagious diffusion in every phase of our common life of methods that are identical with the ends to be reached and that recourse to monistic, wholesale, absolutist procedures is a betrayal of human freedom no matter in what guise it presents itself. An American democracy can serve the world only as it demonstrates in the conduct of its own life the efficacy of plural, partial, and experimental methods in securing and maintaining an ever-increasing release of the powers of human nature, in service of a freedom which is cooperative and a cooperation which is voluntary.

We have no right to appeal to time to justify complacency about the ultimate result. We have every right to point to the long non-democratic and anti-democratic course of human history and to the recentness of democracy in order to enforce the immensity of the task confronting us. The very novelty of the experiment explains the impossibility of restricting the problem to any one element, aspect, or phase of our common everyday life. We have every right to appeal to the long and slow process of time to protect ourselves from the pessimism that comes from taking a short-span temporal view of events—under one condition. We must know that the dependence of ends upon means is such that the only *ultimate* result is the result that is attained today, tomorrow, the next day, and day after day, in the succession of years and generations. Only thus can we be sure that we face our problems in detail one by one as they arise, with all the resources provided by collective intelligence operating in cooperative action. At the end as at the beginning the democratic method is as fundamentally simple and as immensely difficult as is the energetic, unflagging, unceasing creation of an ever-present new road upon which we can walk together.

GREAT BOOKS IN PHILOSOPHY PAPERBACK SERIES

ETHICS

SOCIAL AND POLITICAL PHILOSOPHY

METAPHYSICS/EPISTEMOLOGY

PHILOSOPHY OF RELIGION

ESTHETICS

GREAT MINDS PAPERBACK SERIES

ECONOMICS

RELIGION

SCIENCE

HISTORY

SOCIOLOGY

LITERATURE

(Prices subject to change without notice.)

SPECIAL—For your library . . . the entire collection of 50 "Great Books in Philosophy" and 9 "Great Minds" available at a savings of more than 15%. Only $340.00 for the "Great Books" and $84.00 for the "Great Minds" (plus $12.00 postage and handling). Please indicate "Great Books/Great Minds—Complete Set" on your order form.

The books listed can be obtained from your book dealer or directly from Prometheus Books. Please indicate the appropriate titles. Remittance must accompany all orders from individuals. Please include $3.50 postage and handling for the first book and $1.75 for each additional title (maximum $12.00, NYS residents please add applicable sales tax). Books will be shipped fourth-class book post. **Prices subject to change without notice.**

Send to _____
(Please type or print clearly)

Address _____

City _____ State _____ Zip _____

Amount enclosed _____

Charge my ☐ **VISA** ☐ **MasterCard**

Account # [ ][ ][ ][ ][ ][ ][ ][ ][ ][ ][ ][ ][ ][ ][ ][ ][ ][ ]

Exp. Date _____/_____ Tel.# _____

Signature _____

Prometheus Books Editorial Offices
700 E. Amherst St., Buffalo, New York 14215

Distribution Facilities
59 John Glenn Drive, Amherst, New York 14228

Phone Orders call toll free: (800) 421-0351
FAX: (716) 691-0137
Please allow 3-6 weeks for delivery